ENERGY

EMOTIONS

PEOPLE SKILLS

LIFE FORCE

GENERIC MOTIVATION

SPECIFIC MOTIVATION

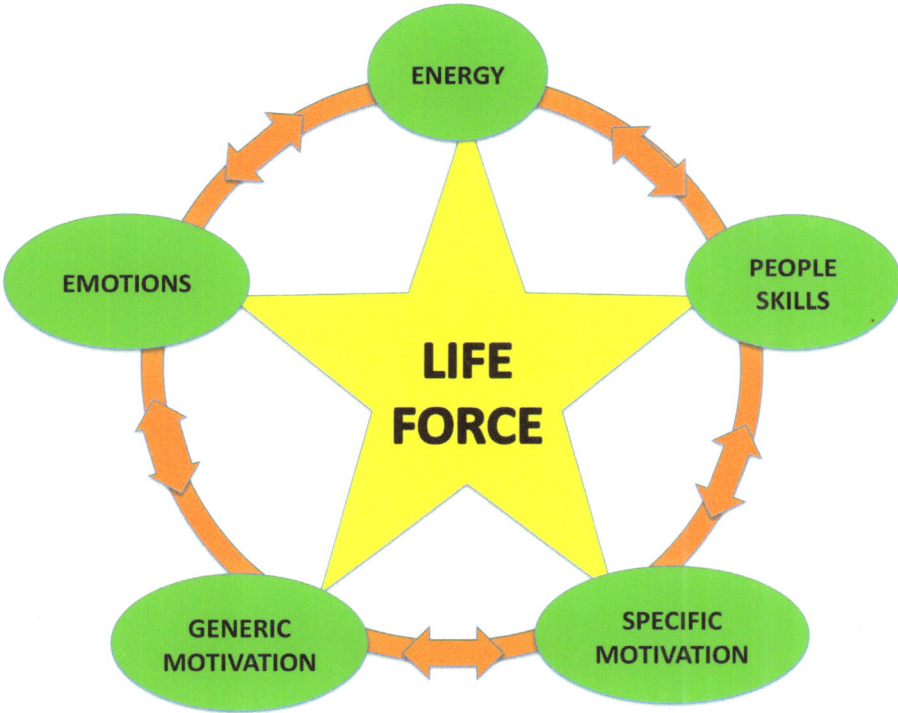

LIFE FORCE
AND THE CIRCLE OF DEPENDENCY

BRIAN MOORE

ABOUT THIS BOOK

This book is about "TOTAL MOTIVATION" and what drives us to behave in the way that we do. It explains the everyday experiences that we have, and how they all relate to each other, hopefully in very simple and easy to understand language.

The book is not based directly on any psychological theories or any of the ancient philosophies. These areas may of course be very important to many people, but they are largely opinions will not apply to all the people all of the time. If they provide comfort, and work for you, they can easily be accommodated within the concepts of this book and how you would define your own particular "LIFE FORCE."

Above all else this book is intended to make you think about how you behave on a day to day basis, in the real world that we live in and also how we should relate to each other in a positive and helpful way.

There are no absolute answers about "What is the meaning of life?" but we should all strive to "Make our life meaningful!"

Hopefully the book is a practical guide for day to day living.

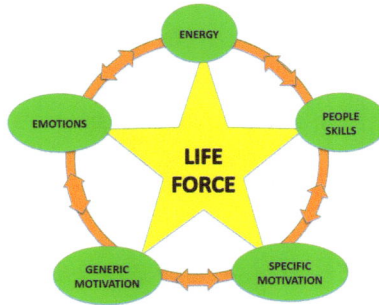

INDEX

CIRCLE OF DEPENDENCY

Motivation is a well studied subject and many books have been written about it. I have read many of them and I have also been privileged to work with many different and exciting people. My conclusion is that real MOTIVATION IS A TOTAL CONCEPT, that is impacted by who we are, what we are, how we feel and what is happening to us. This could be considered as applying to 5 areas that impact our life which I have called "THE CIRCLE OF DEPENDENCY"

5 KEY AREAS IN THE CIRCLE OF DEPENDENCE

GENERIC MOTIVATION. Our environment both physical, social. job and wealth.

ENERGY. This is our basic physical fitness and intelligence.

EMOTIONS. This is the way we respond emotionally to what is happening to us.

PEOPLE SKILLS. The way we communicate and operate with people.

SPECIFIC MOTIVATION. Do we have goals, ambitions, targets

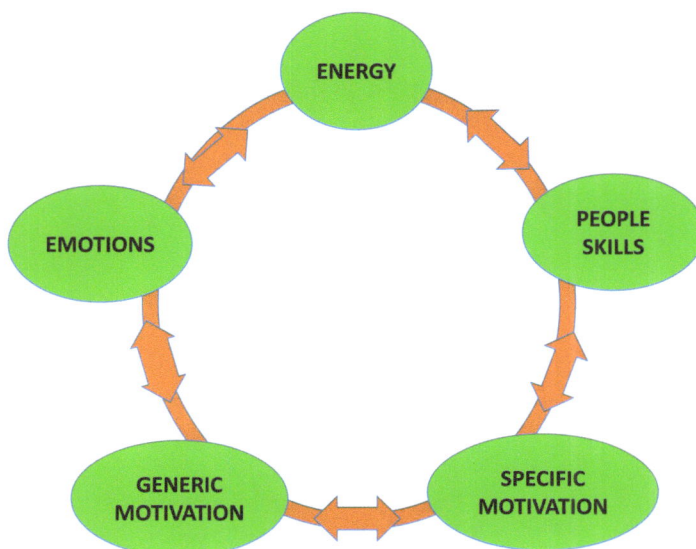

MOTIVATIONAL MODEL A TOTAL CONCEPT
THE LIFE FORCE & CIRCLE OF DEPENDENCY THAT DRIVES US

Thinking about the "Circle of Dependency" it was clear that all these areas are controlled and driven and interact with the "Essential Person" that we each uniquely are. I have defined this inner persona as our "**LIFE FORCE**"

LIFE FORCE is a constantly changing part of us and it controls to a degree how we react to the 5 areas in the circle of dependence.

These 5 KEY AREAS are all important in their own right but they all INTERACT with each other and affect our LIFE FORCE.

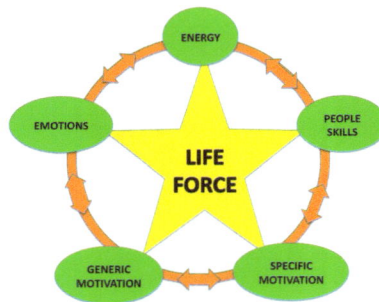

A WAY TO LOOK AT A PERSON

We all have a CIRCLE OF DEPENDENCY and the stronger it is the more it enriches and develops our LIFE FORCE. The weaker the CIRCLE OF DEPENDENCY the more involved our LIFE FORCE becomes in order for us to get things done and function. We operate against the odds as it were. If all else fails we just keep going driven by our LIFE FORCE!

In my view it is the responsibility of everyone to develop their own CIRCLE OF DEPENDENCY and to behave in a way that we support and develop the CIRCLE OF DEPENDENCY of everyone who we come into contact with.

This book will define and discus these 5 KEY AREAS and the LIFE FORCE and how they relate to each other and impact everything we do and how they in turn are also impacted by everything we do.

LIFE FORCE

LIFE FORCE

LIFE FORCE DEFINED

Life force is defined as the way each person behaves and what makes us all unique individuals. It will be different for everyone with respect to its nature and strength. It is what defines us, it is how we drive ourselves. It is the mechanism that we use to manage how the 5 KEY AREAS affect us, or not? It is how people view us. The LIFE FORCE contains so many aspects. Perhaps the three that everyone will recognize are, our ability to think and reason (Brain), our feelings and how we let them rule our decisions (Heart) our thoughts about things that make us think that there is more to this life (Spirit). There are many other features, our judgement, our perception, our prejudices etc. The LIFE FORCE is under constant development but it has certain characteristics that define you. Our **VALUES** and **BELIEFS.** Many clever people have studied what is inside us, what makes us tick?. Just one conclusion. No one really knows all the answers. So as a working assumption the **LIFE FORCE is defined as YOU.** It is what makes you what you are. It is the inner us. Many people will only see how we behave through the 5 KEY areas. Maybe never see the real YOU.

The essential role of the LIFE FORCE is to look at what is happening in the 5 KEY AREAS and to be constantly checking and moving between these areas to ensure that BALANCE is maintained and that we are able to perform effectively. We use our LIFE FORCE to obtain strength from the strong areas in order to deal with any issues in the weak areas. It is important that the CIRCLE OF DEPENDENCY is not breached and that our life force is not over run. You will know if the life force is under attack because thoughts will start to develop in your head like.

I CAN DEAL WITH THIS.

THIS IS NOT GOING TO GET TO ME.

DEVELOPING AND PROTECTING
THE LIFE FORCE

The stronger the life force is then there is less for it to do in order to protect us from any problems in the 5 KEY AREAS. If our Circle of Dependency is continually attacked our life force could become depleted. It may become strengthened (character building through adversity?).

The way we deploy our life force is to look at the areas that may be particularly strong for us and then deploy the strong areas against any of the weak areas where we may have a problem, for example;

The boss upsets you emotionally so you go and have a workout.

You have an emotional upset so you use your people skills to talk it out.

You lose a valuable possession so you use your emotional strength to put it into perspective.

THERE ARE MANY THOUSANDS OF OTHER WAYS.
WHAT WORKS FOR YOU?

Some will work, some will not. The choices that we make on how to deal with the relationship between the 5 key areas is largely determined by our VALUES and BELIEFS.

Everyone will weight the 5 KEY AREAS as having differing levels of importance. Some people will value generic motivation (materialism) very highly and have no real emotional depth. For these people to spend money in a shop because they feel low may make them feel better.

Other people may value spiritual energy and emotions highly, and go and find a spiritual place for quiet reflection and renewal. Know what works for you and for those around you, especially if you are leading them, or are in a relationship with them. We are all different.

ABOVE ALL ELSE DO NOT LET ANYTHING DEPLETE
THE LIFE FORCE BECAUSE

THE LIFE FORCE IS

YOU!

DEFINING THE FIVE IN THE
CIRCLE OF DEPENDENCY AREAS

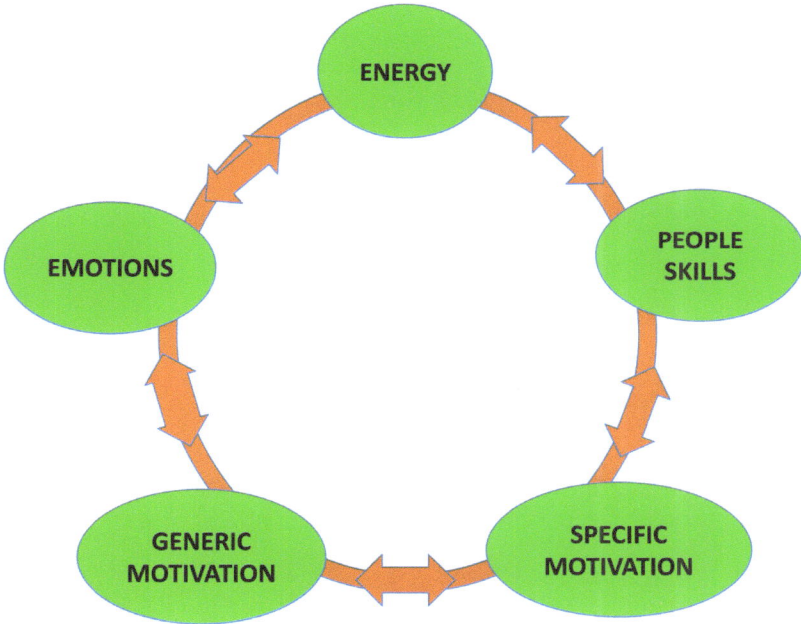

In defining the five areas it should be recognized there will be degrees of overlap. These definitions are broad indications of main characteristics. We are complex and variable creatures!

DEFINITIONS

GENERIC MOTIVATION

The world we live in and our surroundings that provide the basic support system for our motivation. Our material possessions, our job, our social infra structure, the teams we support, our affiliations, college alumni, old friends etc. It will include the geography of where we live and the general environment that we are in on a day to day basis. The evolution of these factors will also shape our thinking.

ENERGY

This is as basic as how fit we are and our skill set. Do we have stamina? Do we have any special attributes physically? That will help us. Athletic ability for example. What is our level of intelligence, is it sufficient to meet the requirements of the world we live in?

EMOTIONS

The window of our emotional state and in particular how we react in situations. Are we EMOTIONAL? Do we have certain responses to certain situations. What is our tolerance for dealing with emotional situations? This area deals with how we react emotionally on a day to day basis to events as they happen. This would not include our LIFE FORCE persona if it had a strong EMOTIONAL characteristic that may define us. For example if we are viewed as a very compassionate person.

DEFINITIONS

PEOPLE SKILLS

Our ability to relate to other people. Are we able to Win friends and influence people? Do we have the social skills to function in the workplace or a community at large? Do we have the skills to communicate our thoughts and feelings to other people? Are we confident in the company of others? Do other people seek out our company?

SPECIFIC MOTIVATION

These are our goals. We have a background of GENERIC MOTIVATION but do we have goals, ambitions and things we would like to do. How driven and motivated are we to achieve our goals and dreams? In the workplace this would be the tasks that we are expected to do. It would also include training to do the SPECIFIC tasks. In the social world this would be our aspirations and plans, such as marriage, children, Travel, etc.

LIFE FORCE

BALANCING ROLE OF THE LIFE FORCE
The 5 areas are formed from our reaction to our experiences and are also under constant influence from external factors. For example, if we lose a valuable possession, we consequently have to use our emotional capacity to put the loss in perspective. The LIFE FORCE is acting as a type of "TRAFFIC COP" watching what is going on in these areas and making sure that we maintain BALANCE in our lives. The LIFE FORCE is also ebbing and flowing as the 5 areas come under differing levels of activity good or bad. The LIFE FORCE also provides back up to the CIRCLE OF DEPENDENCY, which is there to enrich and protect our life force. Conversely our life force is there to ensure that if we have serious problems in any, or all of these five areas it will take over in order to ensure we are still able to function.

FACTORS THAT IMPACT THE 5 KEY AREAS

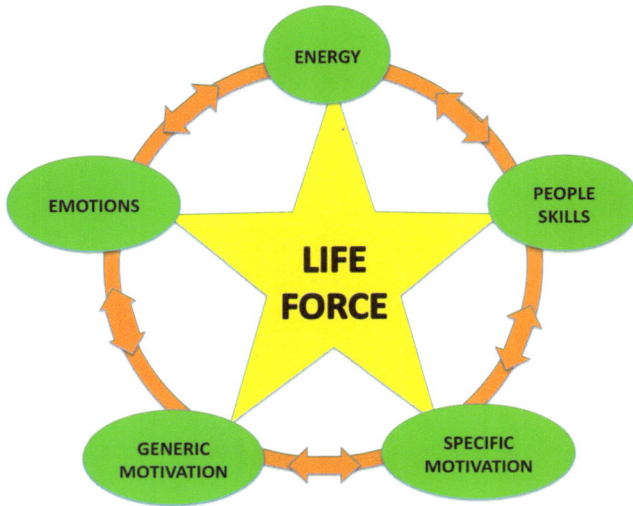

The 5 KEY AREAS are constantly changing which impacts our LIFE force. In turn it has to deal with these changes. This EXPERIENCE affects two fundamental areas.

HOW WE FEEL.

HOW WE ARE SEEN BY OTHERS (ATTITUDE).

FACTORS THAT AFFECT THE 5 KEY AREAS

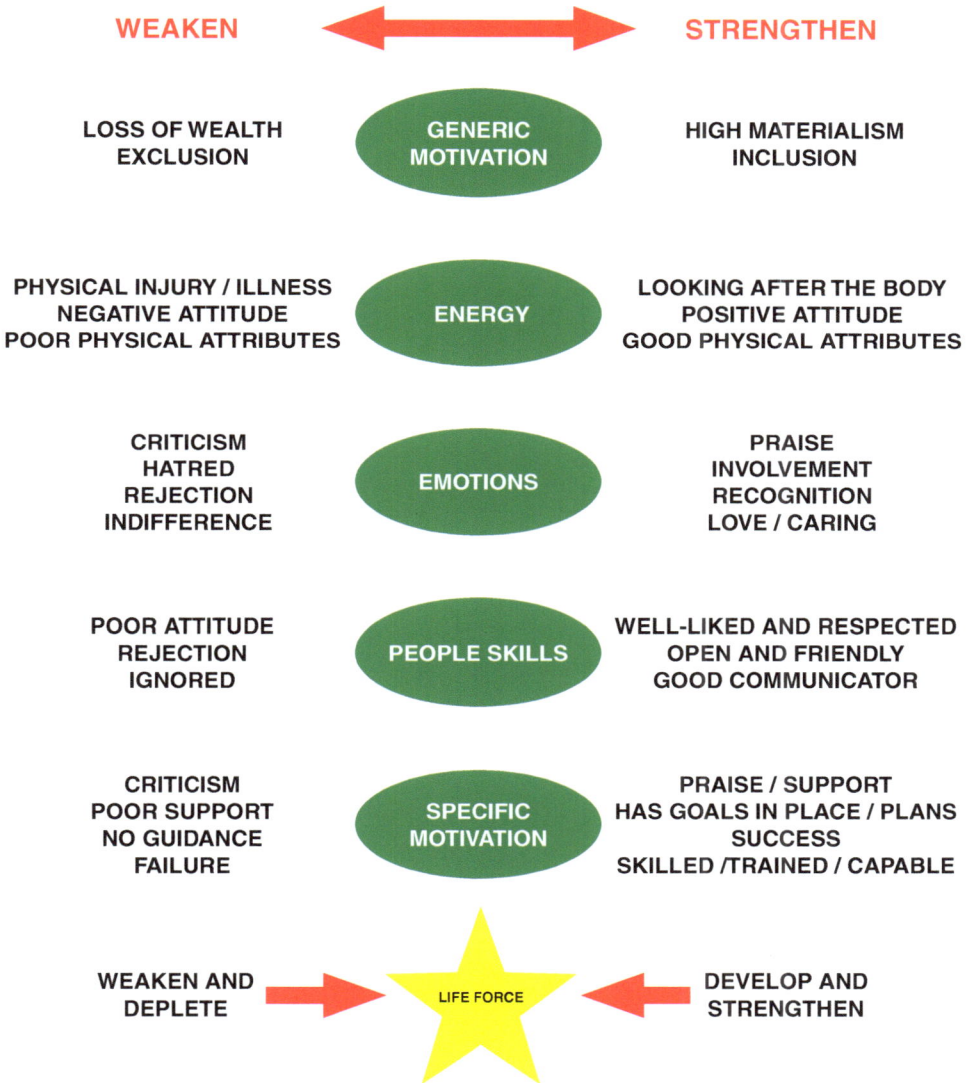

WEAKEN ⟷ STRENGTHEN

WEAKEN		STRENGTHEN
LOSS OF WEALTH EXCLUSION	**GENERIC MOTIVATION**	HIGH MATERIALISM INCLUSION
PHYSICAL INJURY / ILLNESS NEGATIVE ATTITUDE POOR PHYSICAL ATTRIBUTES	**ENERGY**	LOOKING AFTER THE BODY POSITIVE ATTITUDE GOOD PHYSICAL ATTRIBUTES
CRITICISM HATRED REJECTION INDIFFERENCE	**EMOTIONS**	PRAISE INVOLVEMENT RECOGNITION LOVE / CARING
POOR ATTITUDE REJECTION IGNORED	**PEOPLE SKILLS**	WELL-LIKED AND RESPECTED OPEN AND FRIENDLY GOOD COMMUNICATOR
CRITICISM POOR SUPPORT NO GUIDANCE FAILURE	**SPECIFIC MOTIVATION**	PRAISE / SUPPORT HAS GOALS IN PLACE / PLANS SUCCESS SKILLED /TRAINED / CAPABLE
WEAKEN AND DEPLETE ➡	**LIFE FORCE**	⬅ DEVELOP AND STRENGTHEN

HOW WE FEEL!

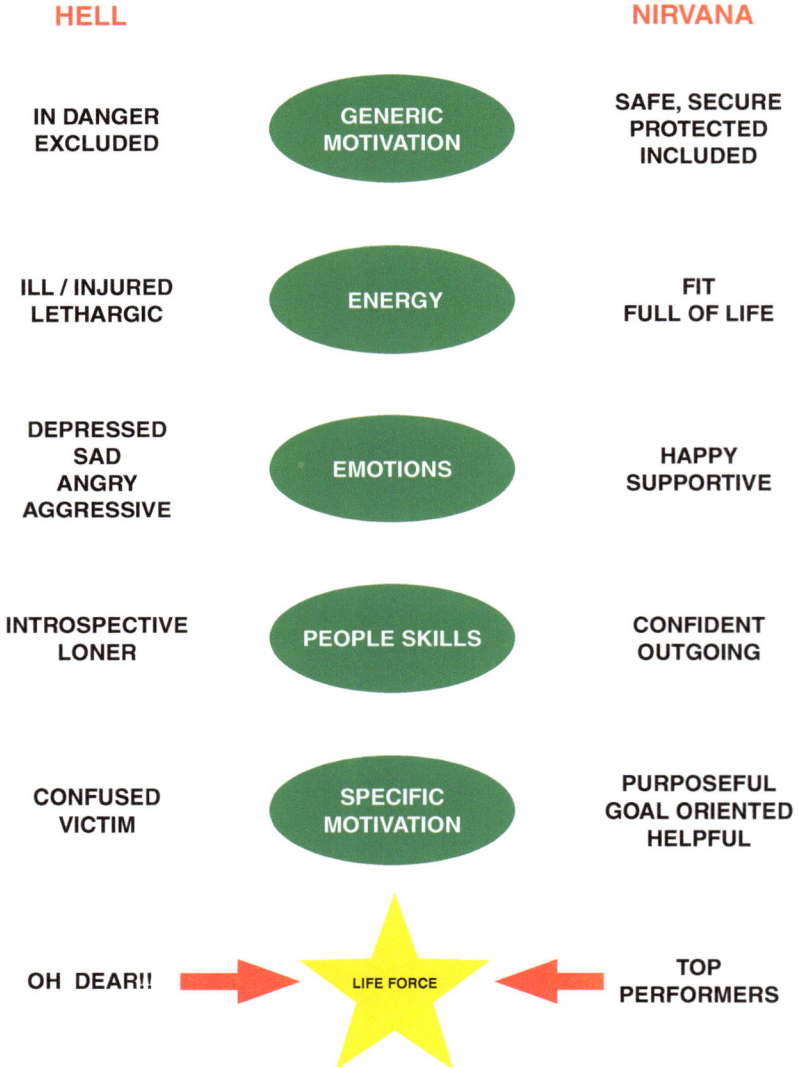

HELL

NIRVANA

IN DANGER
EXCLUDED

GENERIC
MOTIVATION

SAFE, SECURE
PROTECTED
INCLUDED

ILL / INJURED
LETHARGIC

ENERGY

FIT
FULL OF LIFE

DEPRESSED
SAD
ANGRY
AGGRESSIVE

EMOTIONS

HAPPY
SUPPORTIVE

INTROSPECTIVE
LONER

PEOPLE SKILLS

CONFIDENT
OUTGOING

CONFUSED
VICTIM

SPECIFIC
MOTIVATION

PURPOSEFUL
GOAL ORIENTED
HELPFUL

OH DEAR!!

LIFE FORCE

TOP
PERFORMERS

HOW OTHERS PERCEIVE OUR ATTITUDE!

NEGATIVE		POSITIVE
COMPLAINING HIGH MAINTENANCE	GENERIC MOTIVATION	ACCEPTING LOW MAINTENANCE
LETHARGIC	ENERGY	LARGER THAN LIFE
EMOTIONAL CONSTANT DRAMA	EMOTIONS	WELL-BALANCED SENSIBLE
DIFFICULT REQUIRES REMINDING CRITICAL /JUDGMENTAL	PEOPLE SKILLS	OPEN / HONEST SUPPORTIVE TEAM PLAYER
CONFUSED INEFFECTIVE	SPECIFIC MOTIVATION	DRIVEN EFFECTIVE HIGH ACHIEVER
WEAK & A PROBLEM CONFUSED & DIFFICULT	LIFE FORCE	STRONG & ASSERTIVE KNOW WHAT WE WANT

THESE ARE THE LABELS THAT PEOPLE JUDGE US BY. RIGHTLY OR WRONGLY.

THEORIES. A PAUSE TO REFLECT.

I am aware that so many words and ideas to do with people I have not mentioned. Some readers will be trying to establish what ancient theory or psychological research this book is based upon. The answer is none of them. Above all this is intended to be a simple and practical book that relates to the "Human Experience" and is intended to help us to try and lead a more meaningful life and to try and help other people to do the same.

The definition of LIFE FORCE is all inclusive. So I thought that I would list as many theories that I have come across that someone, somewhere thinks may have had an impact on our behavior and who we are? Some from highly reputable studies to some really "Out there stuff."Maybe??

Astrology. When and where we were born. Sun spot activity. A superior force or being built the world in 6 days. If we were breast fed, how our toilet training went. Name worked out in numbers. Chinese years we were born. What happened the first five years of our life. Evolution. Evolved from the monkeys. Our prior life programmed into our DNA and passed down. Foods that our mother may have eaten when carrying us. Fathers age at conception and the quality of the sperm. Alcohol consumed before and after conception. Birthing experience, sequence in the number of children our mother had, Illnesses mother had when carrying us. If mother smoked when carrying us. Reinforcement patterns of behavior that impact personality. Behaving like salivating dogs, ringing bells like conditioned pigeons. After life spirits occupying us. Chemical structure of the brain. Exposure to any harmful toxins when young. How many words we heard in the first few years of our life, music played to us when were in our mothers womb. Descended from space travelers, our DNA arrived on asteroids.

COMPLEX BEINGS ARE WE NOT?

The important point about ALL of these theories is that they are basically opinions. Someone may have done some research. In some cases extensive research. These opinions may well apply to most of the people most of the time. But they are not accepted by all of the people all of the time. Billions of people believe in a superior being that is driving their LIFE FORCE and value system. The "Will of God" or "Inshalla." Everyone will have their own unique set of Values and Beliefs that will define their "LIFE FORCE"

The only one on the list that has some pretty factual support is the theory of evolution. This explains How and when we got here maybe not the Why and What for? I take great comfort in this theory in one particular situation.

When another person is giving you a hard time (as much as you are letting them?) just think this thought. Their descendants used to sit in trees eating bananas and scratching themselves. This mental image may help. Please do not smile at this thought, at the time. This may not be a good idea?

LIFE FORCE DEVELOPMENT

LIFE FORCE

OUR LIFE FORCE EBBS AND FLOWS

DEPENDING UPON OUR EXPERIENCES IN THE CIRCLE OF DEPENDENCY.

We are constantly having different experiences in the 5 KEY AREAS. We use our LIFE FORCE to move between these areas in order to create a good feeling and to negate any feelings that may be not going so well.

For most of us, most of the time, this is an ongoing part of life and we get on with it and survive. "Suffering the slings and arrows of outrageous fortune, "as it were. For some people, some of the time, the 5 KEY AREAS may be under attack, maybe all of them from different aspects. The CIRCLE MAY BECOME OVERWHELMED and our LIFE FORCE IS THREATENED. This is when we start to feel depressed, want to give up, quit, take time off. This can be very serious in us and other people. We should be constantly checking ourselves and checking each other to ensure that our LIFE FORCE is strong and functioning. This is what being a responsible member of the human race is all about, in my view.

GOING FOR GREEN
(A QUICK AUDIT ON HOW WE FEEL?)

UNHAPPY   NOT HAPPY   HAPPY

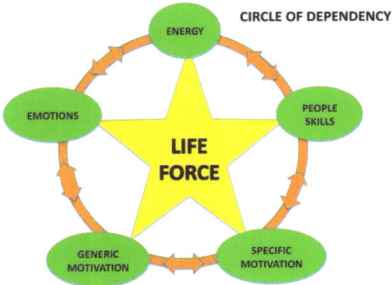

GREAT! EVERYTHING GOING WELL.

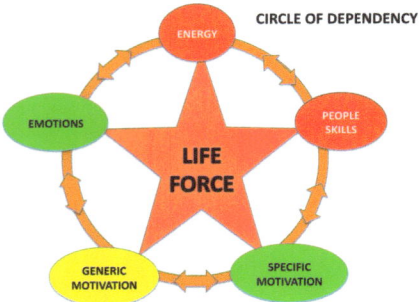

WORK IN PROGRESS.

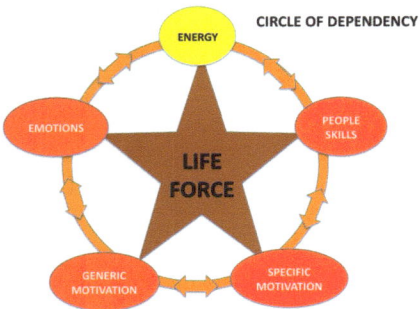

OH DEAR, YOU NEED A SERIOUS CHAT WITH YOURSELF OR SOMEONE?

LIFE FORCE TAKE OVER

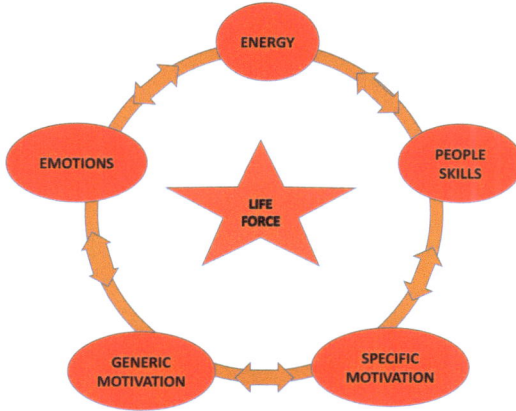

WHEN ALL ELSE FAILS

OUR LIFE FORCE MAY HAVE TO TAKE OVER

Make sure that it is strong enough

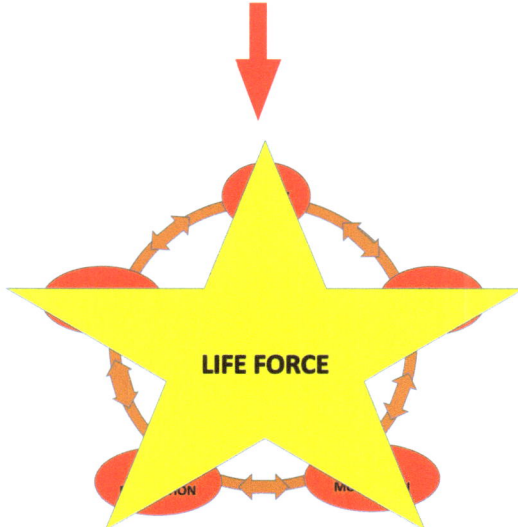

TO SURVIVE

AND START TO REPAIR

DEVELOPING THE AREAS

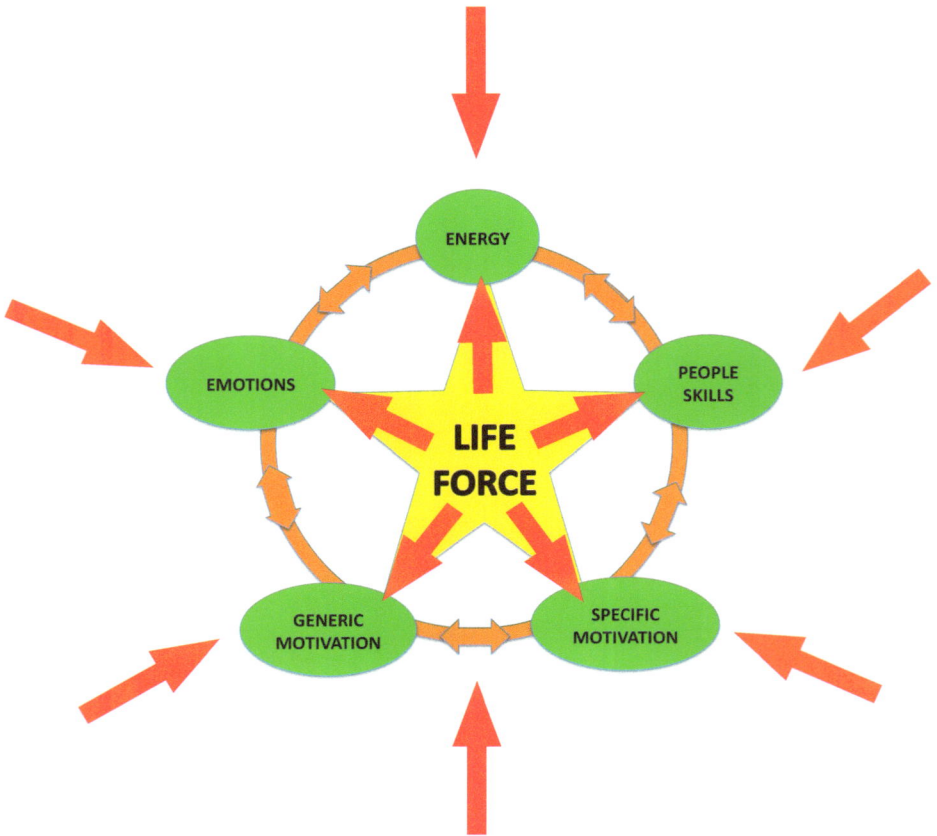

THESE AREAS CAN BE DEVELOPED FROM INSIDE BY OURSELVES AND FROM OUTSIDE BY OUR EXPERIENCES.

DEVELOPING THE AREAS

GENERIC MOTIVATION

THE NEED

This area is to do with the world that you live in, your home, job, friends, wealth geography etc. The greater the variety, stronger your wealth and the more happy that your relationships are then the stronger this area will be. This would be a major strength for some people when in a large and gregarious social setting. Not so much for people who operate in a more solitary mode who only focus on one or two of the five areas. The extreme person is the total loner with virtually no social inclusion regardless of wealth. Some people find many interactions a drain.

SOME IDEAS?

Create wealth through task driven activities mainly work. Usually the wealthier you are the more freedom of action you may have.

This happiness is all well and good, but it does not always bring you wealth.

Look to join clubs and societies to improve your social network. This may also improve your people skills.

Do an audit of your material possessions and decide if you REALLY need them or if they are taking energy and resources to maintain them. Seriously think about a plan to reduce your materialistic footprint (possessions). Unless that is what turns you on, collecting wealth. All about values. You decide.

Make sure that your work is giving you everything you require, or need. Remember it is called "work" for a purpose. It is paid employment and you probably NEED the money. So if you are lucky enough to enjoy your job that's great. But you are not being paid to enjoy yourself. That is a bonus.

**THE STRONGER EACH AREA IS. THE STRONGER THE TOTAL LIFE FORCE IS
THE MORE BALANCED EACH AREA IS, THE MORE RESILIENT THE LIFE FORCE IS.**

DEVELOPING THE AREAS

ENERGY

THE NEED

This looks at if we are fit in mind and body to function. Do we have the basic energy and physical attributes to deal with the world that we live in? Is our intellect and brain power able to meet the demands that are placed on it? This will require constant attention to our most valuable possession. Our "BODY?" The number 1 priority is to have enough energy to function.

SOME IDEAS?

Stay fit at the level appropriate to your needs. This will be different for a professional athlete than an office worker. Develop a "keep fit" routine that works for you. The more fit you are then the happier the world is, usually?

Watch what you eat and drink. Diets do not work. You have to develop a lifestyle of eating and drinking that will enable your body to function at the level that you require it to. Eat less,(we all eat far too much). Watch alcohol intake, and try to eat loads of fruit and vegetables as they are the closest thing to the human body in nature. Vegetables and fruits have approximately the same water content as we do therefore they are easier for our body to consume. We use a lot of energy digesting food. The easier that food is to digest then the less of our energy it will take. The last point is that small meals taken often are better than large infrequent meals. As you get older (past the middle years), your food intake should be drastically reduced and your weight carefully monitored.

Have a regular physical check up on the basics. Listen to what your body is telling you. I was discussing this with a doctor at one of the major clinics and he said that our body well tell us through the way we feel if there is something wrong. Any major change in the way we feel should be investigated. This does not include if some really nasty bug or virus just gets in, that's bad luck. I am talking about general disposition and progressive illnesses.

Keep the brain active. Use mental exercises to give it a regular workout it. Like your body.

THE STRONGER EACH AREA IS. THE STRONGER THE TOTAL LIFE FORCE IS
THE MORE BALANCED EACH AREA IS. THE MORE RESILIENT THE LIFE FORCE IS.

DEVELOPING THE AREAS

EMOTIONS

THE NEED

Here we get into difficult and complex territory. Just exactly what drives our emotional make up, and why it is so changeable. The first thing to say is that if you are really worried about your emotional health get some professional advice. This section is based on some of my observations and personal experience in this area. It is, however clear, that we all have a different emotional make so it is a matter of degree. Some people will become physically moved by a situation, others will just move on and become detached. I think we all have a pretty good idea of our own emotional disposition and its capacity to CHANGE, which it will as life's experiences impact us. We may become softer, or harder or more detached. Depends what is going on in our lives.

SOME IDEAS?

Sleep is very important. When you are tired the world seems a different place. Be aware of long term fatigue as it will creep up on you and you will slowly wind down. When you are really tired you may not care. Basic worries take on a larger than life persona.

Develop some relaxing techniques. Meditate or take an afternoon nap.

Try and avoid needy and emotional people, they will bring you down. We obviously have friends and family who may need us on occassion, or we may need them? Emotional energy is catching, good and bad.

If you are on any form of medication, for anything, read the small print and check it out on the internet. It may have emotional side effects that you are unaware of. This also applies to some food stuffs that may affect you. Watch the amount of alcohol you drink. It can be a depressant that may last a few days, I don't mean the hangover. We all have a different bio chemical make up and react to everything that comes into our body in a different way. Look for patterns and symptoms and check if you are allergic to anything.

THE STRONGER EACH AREA IS. THE STRONGER THE TOTAL LIFE FORCE IS THE MORE BALANCED EACH AREA IS. THE MORE RESILIENT THE LIFE FORCE IS.

DEVELOPING THE AREAS

PEOPLE SKILLS

THE NEED

Most people think the skilled "People Person" is the gregarious, out going person, all things to all people, confident and relaxed in any situation and able to talk to anybody any where. Of course, if you are like this and you are genuine (very important) then you have a distinct advantage. But if you are not like that then there are a few tips that can really help. They are easy to understand but difficult to do.

BASIC PEOPLE SKILLS

Forget about **you** and focus on the other person.

A persons favorite sound is their "NAME"
Favorite subject is "THEM".

Listening is the most relevant and under rated skill.

Never say anything bad about anybody, anywhere at any time.

Give out praise and positive comments as often as possible
and for as many people as you can.

IF YOU CAN DO ALL THAT.
YOU ARE PROBABLY VISITING FROM ANOTHER PLANET.
SO WELCOME!

THE STRONGER EACH AREA IS. THE STRONGER THE TOTAL LIFE FORCE IS
THE MORE BALANCED EACH AREA IS. THE MORE RESILIENT THE LIFE FORCE IS.

DEVELOPING THE AREAS

SPECIFIC MOTIVATION

THE NEED

These are the specific things that we actively set out to achieve or maybe are given to us to achieve in the workplace. Some people are more task focused and DRIVEN. Other people just get on with it. I like the old saying, "Some people make things happen," "Some people things happen to" and "Some people wondered what happened to them? Which group are you in? A prime mover or victim? Prime movers have goals and go for them. Remember success is about averages not winning all the time. This is not possible. Take comfort from sales people. The very best sales people usually never close more than 50% of the opportunities that they follow up on. This means that they have more failures than successes.But they are viewed as being very successful. As an aside the sales person has to be strong in the emotional and energy areas to deal with the constant rejection and failure. That's just the good ones.

SOME IDEAS?

You can always do better than you think you are capable of.

But, be realistic.

Understand that some of the qualities for success are unsung and below the radar. "Perseverance" and "Patience." It is not all action packed stuff.

Success breeds success and it is contagious. Surround yourself with successful people.

THE STRONGER EACH AREA IS. THE STRONGER THE TOTAL LIFE FORCE IS THE MORE BALANCED EACH AREA IS. THE MORE RESILIENT THE LIFE FORCE IS.

PEOPLE SKILLS

A REALLY USEFUL TIP THAT YOU WILL IGNORE

We all talk about each other behind each others backs, good and bad. Not every one likes everyone. The nature of people is that negative and bad views are usually more interesting. (There is something not too displeasing about the misfortunes of our friends..... William Shakespeare)

THE TIP
Never say anything bad about anybody, any time, anywhere to anybody.

There are absolutely never any upsides from sending negative comments out.

WHY

The person that you are talking to may well go away and reflect and think.
"What do you say about them behind their back?"
You could even get a reputation for being a very negative person.
The person that you are talking about will usually get to
hear about it and that's some support that you may have lost.
Negative thoughts deplete your own emotional energy. Move on, be positive.

If the person thinks equally the same about you. Which they often do. Then when they hear that you have said something positive about them they may well become a supporter. It is hard to not like someone who says nice things about you. Everyone likes to hear "I met so and so the other day, he is a big fan of yours. "EVERY SINGLE ONE OF US LIKES TO HEAR THAT!"

This is probably the single biggest people skill that you could develop.
Will you?

NOT A CHANCE !!

ROAD BLOCKS
EGO / PRIDE / EMOTIONS / PREJUDICES/STUBBORNNESS
ACCEPTING THAT WE MAY BE WRONG

REALLY GREAT QUALITIES TO REALIZE THAT YOU HAVE.

SELF HELP BOOKS

This page may save you a lot of reading.

As one of my heroes would say, "The title is a good start." Its not self help, if you require a book. It is HELP. The vast majority of these books are based on a few principles which if you have the self discipline to follow then you do not need to read another self help book except to remain topical. This is more of a "Fashion" industry than you may realize.

TIPS THAT HELP

YOU. Are the only person that can fix YOU.

Watch what you eat and drink

Take exercise and look after your weight and blood pressure

Get an annual physical that checks for the basic things.

Be nice to people and treat them with respect

Realize that you can do more than you probably think

Be realistic about your expectations

Do not be judgmental

Socialize and be happy

Laugh. Especially at your self. A very funny subject usually.

Be a responsible citizen and member of the human race

Try and have BALANCE in your life

Live within your financial means. Watch debt. Especially credit cards.

Do not take your self too seriously

If some form of spiritual activity works for YOU. Do it.

Respect other persons views, beliefs and spiritual persona.

Try and live in the NOW.

CHECKING OUT OUR AREAS

Our LIFE FORCE the essential "**YOU**" is constantly reviewing what is happening in our life and this is reflected in our general disposition. Do we feel Good? Are we Happy, are we just NOT HAPPY or are we really UNHAPPY. We can usually put up with being NOT HAPPY for some time but if we are UNHAPPY then CHANGES MAY BE REQUIRED. We should be constantly evaluating the five areas to see what is causing us to feel the way we are. Is it work, Our health, Our personal life? Try not to rely on any one area as so many people do. Try to keep a BALANCE. This provides the LIFE FORCE with extra resilience in dealing with any problems.

SOME SIGNS THAT ALL MAY NOT BE WELL.
Difficulty sleeping, eating too much or not enough.
Changes in our body, (Weight, skin, lethargy. Loss of appetite.)
People are re acting aggressively to you.
Making more mistakes than usual, a bit more accident prone.
You can only see negative thoughts, everything in the world is bad.
Drinking heavily.
Becoming impatient and restless.
You have no wealth.

THESE COULD BE DANGER SIGNS THAT THE LIFE FORCE MAY BE IN DISTRESS. IT MAY BE UNDER STRESS AND IS COMING TO TERMS WITH HOW TO DEAL WITH SOME SERIOUS ISSUES. IN ONE OR MORE OF THE AREAS.

CHECKING OUT OUR AREAS

It would be unusual for all our areas to be going really well all the time. The nature of life is that we all suffer setbacks in some areas of our life at some time. When this happens we rely on the strong areas of our life to compensate for maybe the problem in a weak area. This page gives a few examples of how to do that. There are of course many more. Such is the Human Spirit and the strength of our LIFE FORCE which will be CONTROL-LING this INTERNAL HELP PROCESS. Our VALUE systems will play a large part in what the LIFE FORCE will deploy to protect an area that is weak.

EXAMPLES OF INTERNAL SUPPORT

We have been upset. So we use our people skills to talk to a friend.

We feel emotionally low and depressed so we do something physical.

We feel low so we go and spend some money on a shopping spree.

We feel life is drifting so we focus more on our goals and plans.

We go somewhere quiet for reflection and thought.

We feel the need to go and help someone to get a feel good factor.

We lose our Job so we become active in job seeking.

IF ALL ELSE FAILS THE LIFE FORCE TAKES OVER TO SURVIVE

LIFE FORCE

THEN IT HAS TO "REPAIR" THE DAMAGE!

COMMUNICATING

The way we communicate is through the 5 areas. What and how we communicate is largely defined by our LIFE FORCE. It will decide where ever possible who sees what about us, when they see it and how they see us. Certain things are obvious and will be communicated by our presence and the way we move and relate to other people. Our value system will affect all of the communications but our deeply held values may only be shown to a few special people. If anyone at all!

Actions speak louder than words

What we do signals our value system and priorities.

We should aim to do as we say and say as we do.

We can become defined by our communication patterns. Always late? Never return calls? Etc. People start to predict your behavior, good and bad, from how you communicate and behave (Which is communication).

**In everything we say and do.
We are communicating.**

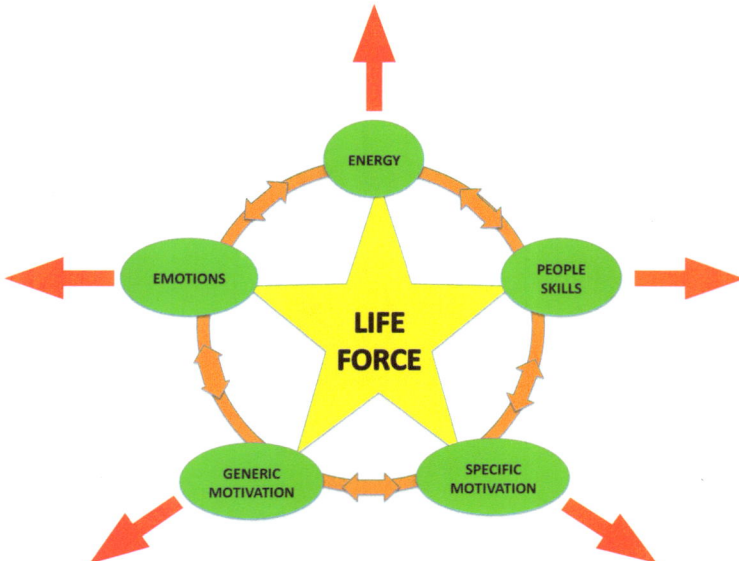

COMMUNICATING THROUGH THE AREAS

GENERIC MOTIVATION

WHAT WE SEND OUT

WHAT WE MAY GET BACK (Good and Bad)

Where we live

The box that you live in.
Defines the box that people may put you in!

What we wear

GOOD. Admiration. Respect.
BAD. Resentment. Judgement.

Our job

GOOD. Admiration, respect. Job offers.
BAD. Resentment. Judgement. Requests for help.

Vehicle that we drive

GOOD. Admiration. Respect.
BAD. Judgement. Speeding tickets. Big bills.
Attract unwanted attention.

Our circle of friends

GOOD. Bonding with like minded people.
Fulfillment. Opportunities to do other things.
BAD. Envy, jealousy resentment. A friend in need
can be a big problem (did I get that quote right?)

The organizations
we belong to

GOOD. Bonding with like minded people.
Fulfillment. A sense of purpose. An opportunity to
develop friends and skills.
BAD. Envy. Jealousy. Resentment.

Our religion and
worshiping practices

GOOD. A deep sense of spiritual satisfaction with
like minded people. Fulfillment
BAD. Envy, jealousy resentment. Ridicule. Acts of
violence.

COMMUNICATING THROUGH THE AREAS

ENERGY

WHAT WE SEND OUT	WHAT WE MAY GET BACK (Good and Bad)
Working out	**GOOD.** Sense of well being as ENDORPHINS are released. Sense of achievement. A better body and maybe a longer life. **BAD.** Injuries.
What you eat and drink	**Your body.** You are what you eat and drink!
How long you sleep	I have given up on that one. Its somewhere between 8 and five hours a night depending on your age and which phase the moon is in. Rest is however fundamental
How we think	**GOOD**. Admiration. Bonding. **BAD.** Criticism.
Working long hours	**GOOD.** Appreciation and success. Avoiding all the boring stuff in life. A lot of money. **BAD.** Pity for being a sad workaholic. No social life, lose friends. A divorce, family pass you by. Burnt out, stress illness.
Very good Looking/ Attractive	**GOOD**. More success at work, attract attention. **BAD.** Resented attacked, unwanted attention. Desire to be left alone. Desire to be treated as normal. My phone number!
Lethargic slow moving	**BAD.** Run over. Ignored. **GOOD.** Left alone.
Willing, enthusiastic and supportive	**GOOD.** A sense of well being for being such a great helpful person. More work. Promotion. **BAD.** Being taken advantage of.

COMMUNICATING THROUGH THE AREAS

EMOTIONS

WHAT WE SEND OUT

WHAT WE MAY GET BACK (Good and Bad)

Happy disposition
Joy /Excited

GOOD. Energized and happy people.
BAD. Skeptical thoughts.

Angry looks

BAD. Avoidance. Maybe questions. People feeling guilty! What did I do?

Indifference

BAD. Avoidance. Maybe questions.

Worried and concerned
Depressed

GOOD. Sympathy
BAD. Questions why? Offers of help,. Being avoided.

Compassion

GOOD. Feel good, People using it and/or appreci-ating it.
BAD. Being taken advantage of.

Guilt

BAD. Arrested! Avoidance. People wondering what you did

Hate

BAD. Hate and Pity.

Aggression

BAD. Damaged people. Meet a psychiatrist. Physical damage.

Crying

GOOD. Sympathy, tissue, help.
BAD. Embarrassment, avoidance.

FEAR/SCARED

This is so damaging and can lead to the most debilitating activity that we engage in "WORRY". This in turn can lead to anxiety and depression. A very dangerous progression of emotions. This is so important that I have dedicated a whole page to FEAR. (Page70)

COMMUNICATING THROUGH THE AREAS

PEOPLE SKILLS

WHAT WE SEND OUT

A smile

Their NAME. Favorite subject. THEM.

Pleasant greetings, positive thoughts

Polite and respectful requests for help

Passing on knowledge and experience

Criticism

Hostile words

Silence

Unreasonable requests

An apology

WHAT WE MAY GET BACK (Good and Bad)

GOOD. Hopefully one back? The universal language.

GOOD. A new friend. Free drinks see Charmaine story at back

GOOD. Pleasant greetings, positive thoughts.
BAD. Skeptical looks

GOOD. Help.
BAD. Ignorance.

GOOD. Respect and maybe money if its your job

BAD. Resentment and hostility. Appreciation of your honesty. **Just to be clear no one ever likes criticism what ever they say!**

BAD. Hostile words. Physical violence. Resentment. Being ignored. Or my favorite "A Smile" Depends how you do it?

BAD. Silence. Concerned reactions. People over compensating to please. People wanting to know what's wrong.

GOOD. Maybe a result.
BAD. An argument. Criticisms about your value system.

GOOD. Appreciation. A person with nothing further to say, maybe?

COMMUNICATING THROUGH THE AREAS

SPECIFIC MOTIVATION

YOU or in a TEAM

WHAT WE SEND OUT

Achieving results

Failing to achieve results

Chasing unrealistic goals

No goals

No skills, no training,
no motivation

WHAT WE MAY GET BACK (Good and Bad)

GOOD. Admiration, respect, envy, satisfaction and rewards.
BAD. Jealousy, competition, hostility.

GOOD. Satisfaction of trying. Support. Determination to do better. Empathy. Become more humble and realistic. Laughter.
BAD. Depression and a sense of failure.

GOOD. Higher level of determination? Reality check to adjust the target.
BAD. Frustration, depression and anger. Damaging the balance of your life as the task takes over all other activities.

GOOD. Happiness and contentment? A feeling of superiority watching everyone else chasing the moon!
BAD. Sense of failure

What's on the television?
GOOD. Or more seriously, a desire to get some.

Win some lose some.

VERY GOOD!
Welcome to the human race.

HELPING OTHER PEOPLE

ANOTHER PERSON ➡️

WHY

You will probably feel good about it.

It is a life skill that you should develop.

You may need help yourself one day.

Serendipity may happen? Unintended consequences. Remember the famous restaurant owner who sat out side his restaurant acting as a homeless person. Anyone that showed him kindness received a great free meal. Remember that, when the next homeless person asks for money!

It is an opportunity to spread your energy.
Energy is very contagious and spreads easily!

PLUS.

IT'S THE RIGHT THING TO DO!

HOW WE CAN USE OUR AREAS.
TO HELP AND DEVELOP OTHER PEOPLES AREAS?

HELPING OTHERS

GENERIC MOTIVATION

FROM US   **TO ANOTHER PERSON**

AREAS TO HELP

Gifts and wealth

Social inclusion/Meet new people

Training help.

Like minded support

Networking

BENEFITS

Feel good.

More friends / Feel Good.

May make your life easier

Opportunity to bond

Helping the world go round by meeting lots of people that could maybe help each other

Throwing away money

A Chinese friend coined this phrase for me. Reasonably wealthy good Christian Guy. He used to carry small amounts of money to "throw away" just to help the world go round. Not get worried about small things like a cab driver taking you for a ride in both senses of the word! Over tipping in restaurants etc. His way of quietly just "Paying something back"

Feel good factor.
A lesson in human nature.

Amusement, the look on a cab drivers face that has clearly just pulled a fast one so you tell them and then give them a good tip. The confused look is priceless. Much better than an argument and the feeling of being cheated for an hour or two.

Suspicion. My friend offered to pay for a waitress in a restaurant who we had just met to go to a training course maybe $250? She refused because she could not believe that anyone would just do that with no strings attached?

Passing on praise and compliments   **Always good. Always works.**

HELPING OTHERS

ENERGY

FROM US

TO ANOTHER PERSON

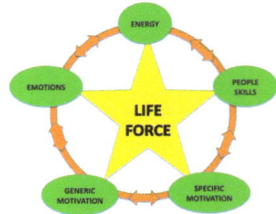

AREAS TO HELP	BENEFITS
Presence can maybe inspire.	Admiration and feel good.
Physically help with work	Keep fit. Feel good. Paid in money or kind
Listen and support when someone is low. People frequently have depleted energy. They may at times want the comfort of taking your energy to help them.	Feel good. Create a stronger friendship bond. Maybe have some one there for you when you want the favor returned. Just wrote that and thought I probably do not agree with the reciprocating comment. In my experience there are "natural givers" who are full of energy and have a strong LIFE FORCE and "natural takers" where the opposite may apply. They still could be very good friends of course for a whole host of other reasons (Givers like to Give and takers like, need? to take). But the larger than life givers usually have a way of getting themselves back on track before the takers have even realized that there may have been a problem.
Drive them to hospital.	It happens?
Cover some of their jobs / Work.	Do stuff for them. Feed the cat when away.

HELPING OTHERS

EMOTIONS

FROM US   **TO ANOTHER PERSON**

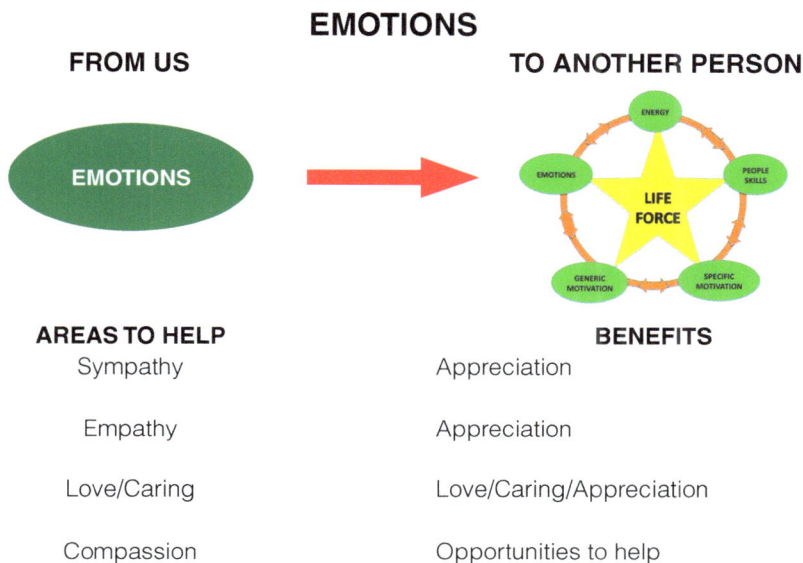

AREAS TO HELP   **BENEFITS**

Sympathy   Appreciation

Empathy   Appreciation

Love/Caring   Love/Caring/Appreciation

Compassion   Opportunities to help

Leave them alone. More effective than you may think. Sometimes we just have to allow time for someone to sort themselves out, accept things, come to terms with what is happening to them.

Time to your self!

Not give advice. Only answer any factual questions. Sometimes people just want to tell you and talk. It is a way of helping themselves come to terms with what ever is causing a problem. Try and avoid diving in with the "What you need to do is…" comments. Men and woman are very different in this area. Women need to talk, men want solutions. (The only comment about the sexes in the book! but it is so true.)

Appreciation

Get help. Sometimes people need professional help.

Some one to help you. Less worry for you maybe?

HELPING OTHERS

PEOPLE SKILLS
FROM US
TO ANOTHER PERSON

AREAS TO HELP	BENEFITS
Listening	Appreciation
Giving advice	Only if you must. Normally not appreciated or accepted. People have to usually find out the hard way. They may well come back after the experience and say "I know what you mean now!" Please just smile and say nothing when that happens.
Giving them information	Feel good. Knowledge, you may be wrong and they will correct you or add to your knowledge.
Answering questions	Appreciation or hostility or resentment. See section on giving advice
Praising them	Praise back. They tell everyone what a great person you are. (For having the talent to recognize how wonderful they are!!) A little cynicism sneaked in there. Funny.
Telling them to read the book "How to win friends and influence people"	**A changed person. Well maybe?**

HELPING OTHERS

SPECIFIC MOTIVATION

FROM US   **TO ANOTHER PERSON**

AREAS TO HELP	BENEFITS
Working on projects together	Help and bonding.
Include them in your team	Team spirit, support and help
Train them Pass on skills.	Satisfaction. Plus save you time. "The not giving you a fish I caught, but I will train you to fish" more time up front but you do not have to fish for them for ever?
Help them set goals. Show them some of the techniques. Like how to do a Mind Map/Brain Path	May help tidy up some of your goals and thinking as you go through the processes
Praise and encourage to succeed.	Appreciation and hopefully will do the same for you?
Comfort a person when they have failed. Give them the "It is not the end of the world speech"	Friendship and appreciation.
A reality check. Some times, some people just need to be sat down and given a "This is how it is talk"	You may lose a friend. But not all of our goals involve friends. Discrete, one on one, with a positive attitude please. Do not let your emotions, like anger or frustration get in the way. No grudges, no recriminations just do it and move on.

Appreciation

What is wonderful in others, becomes a part of you.

CHANGE

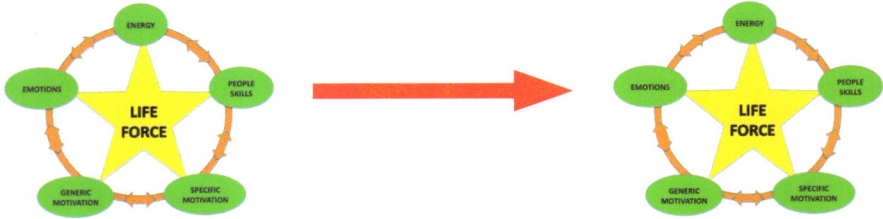

The biggest test that our LIFE FORCE and the CIRCLE OF DEPENDENCY face is how we react to and deal with change. Constant change is a fact of life but the only constant in your life is YOU. How you deal with the various changes that you are faced with will depend upon how that change impacts the areas in your CIRCLE OF DEPENDENCY and how your LIFE FORCE handles those changes. This will depend upon your value system and how important the change is to you. The LIFE FORCE will essentially be evaluating two things. What will I be losing from the CIRCLE OF DEPENDENCY and what will be replacing it. Your LIFE FORCE consequently has to deal with two actions, LOSS and ADJUSTING TO THE NEW SITUATION. Everyone will have a different answer to these questions depending upon the STRENGTH and BALANCE of their CIRCLE OF DEPENDENCY and LIFE FORCE. Some Examples

JOB CHANGE. It could be your main activity and maybe you will not get another job as good. Then if it was not your idea and it is the main strength in your CIRCLE OF DEPENDENCY then this is will be a major traumatic event in your life. If on the other hand it is your idea and you are leaving for a new and more exciting challenge this will probably be a positive and enriching experience.

END OF A RELATIONSHIP. If this is the center of your world and a long term loving and caring partnership of several years then this will be a major traumatic change that you have to deal with, and maybe never recover from? If you are in an abusive and unhappy relationship then this could be period of release and an opportunity to move on.

LOSS / THEFT OF A POSSESSION. If this is your prized car that you worship and value as your pride and joy then this will be a traumatic event? If you just see a car as a means of transport and obtain fulfillment in other activities then this will be a minor inconvenience.

THE POINT

When faced with dealing with CHANGE it is not the event that will drive how it affects you it is how that event impacts your CIRCLE OF DEPENDENCY and LIFE FORCE. An important difference.

THE ADVICE

Be prepared for CHANGE. Nothing is for ever. Make sure that your CIRCLE OF DEPENDENCY and LIFE FORCE is balanced, strong and resilient. Change will not only be easier to deal with but maybe something that you will embrace with a positive attitude.

RELATIONSHIPS

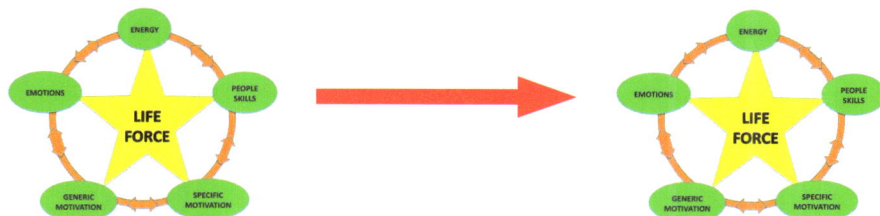

The Holy Grail "How to have many successful relationships" There are no easy answers just questions. To develop a relationship there are certain stages that you have to go through. First, the initial reason for getting together. Then getting to know each other, which is largely reviewing the 5 areas for each person and deciding upon the BALANCE and COMPATIBILITY between them. Finally if these areas are in tune then we have to choose if we are to allow our LIFE FORCES to meet and check out the compatibilities between the innermost them and us.

In some relationships this process may temporarily be reversed. The two LIFE FORCES feel instant attraction and may bond and mate immediately because of the power and chemistry of that attraction. Maybe driven by lust? Then when this wanes which in most relationships is after one or two years then the CIRCLES have to be reviewed to see if the relationship can go further. At this stage CHOICES have to be made. Do I want this to work? If the answer is yes, make sure some of that early "magic" comes out once in a while. This not only applies to interpersonal relationships. Another example would be to join a club or organization after an initial burst of enthusiasm but as our CIRCLE comes to terms with the membership our views and membership may change.

The next few pages outline some common relationships and some sample questions that may help with establishing BALANCE and COMPATIBILITY

In reviewing these questions remember two things.

There are no **RIGHT** and **WRONG** ANSWERS

**IN ALL RELATIONSHIPS THERE IS
ONE REALLY KEY QUESTION.**

DOES IT WORK FOR YOU?

RELATIONSHIP QUESTIONS
AT WORK WITH BOSS

← →

PERSON 1	COMPATIBILITY & BALANCE Sample questions! Many more!	PERSON 2

GENERIC MOTIVATION

Working conditions acceptable,
feel safe and secure?
Pay & benefits Ok ?
Do you feel included and
want to go to work?

GENERIC MOTIVATION

ENERGY

Are you fit to do the job?
Do you have any signs of stress or illness?
Do you find the work stimulating?

ENERGY

EMOTIONS

Do you feel happy and content?
Does anything make you depressed or
Angry ?
Do you have a sense of worth and value?

EMOTIONS

PEOPLE SKILLS

Are you able to talk and relate to
those around you?
Do you understand the language used?
Do you feel part of the team at a
social level?

PEOPLE SKILLS

SPECIFIC MOTIVATION

Do you know clearly what is
expected of you?
Are you trained to do the job?
Are you satisfied with the recognition
you receive?

SPECIFIC MOTIVATION

LIFE FORCE

IF YOU FEEL GOOD ABOUT THESE
QUESTIONS THEN

**Do you feel valued, included,
respected and appreciated?**

LIFE FORCE

RELATIONSHIP QUESTIONS
CLOSE PERSONAL RELATIONSHIP

PERSON 1

COMPATIBILITY & BALANCE
Sample questions! Many more!

PERSON 2

GENERIC MOTIVATION

Do we have the same beliefs and values?
Are we from a similar
socio/economic group?

GENERIC MOTIVATION

ENERGY

Do we have the energy to
meet each others needs?
Can I meet the expectations of my partner?
Do we have the same values for
eating and drinking?

ENERGY

EMOTIONS

Do we love/care for each other ?
Do we have similar emotional
expectations of each other?

EMOTIONS

PEOPLE SKILLS

Do I like the way the other person
talks and treats me?
Do I like the way the other person
relates to people?

PEOPLE SKILLS

SPECIFIC MOTIVATION

Do we want the same outcome
from the relationship?
Are our life goals similar?
Am I happy with the other persons
individual goals?

SPECIFIC MOTIVATION

LIFE FORCE

**IF YOU FEEL GOOD ABOUT THESE
QUESTIONS THEN**

**Do you feel valued, included,
respected and appreciated?**

LIFE FORCE

RELATIONSHIP QUESTIONS
CLOSE SOCIAL RELATIONSHIP

PERSON 1   **COMPATIBILITY & BALANCE**   **PERSON 2**
Sample questions! Many more!

GENERIC MOTIVATION

Are the financial costs the same for both of us?
Do we have same shared interests?
Are the logistics convenient?

GENERIC MOTIVATION

ENERGY

Are we able to meet and do things together?
Do we have the same intellect?

ENERGY

EMOTIONS

Is this enriching, or depleting me?
Are there any emotional issues?
Do we have the same expectations from the relationship?

EMOTIONS

PEOPLE SKILLS

Do I like the way the other person talks to my friends?
Are we able to communicate freely?
Do I feel that the relationship is honest?

PEOPLE SKILLS

SPECIFIC MOTIVATION

Do we want the same things out of the relationship?
Do we want to go to the same places?

SPECIFIC MOTIVATION

LIFE FORCE

IF YOU FEEL GOOD ABOUT THESE QUESTIONS THEN

Do you feel valued, included, respected and appreciated?

LIFE FORCE

RELATIONSHIP REVIEW. ALL RELATIONSHIPS

PERSON 1   HAPPY   NOT HAPPY   UNHAPPY   **PERSON 2**

GENERIC MOTIVATION

WHEN DECIDING
NO WHAT Ifs? OR ALLOWANCES!
JUST SAY HOW YOU "FEEL"
IN EACH AREA

GENERIC MOTIVATION

ENERGY

IF THE OTHER PERSON AGREES
TO COOPERATE
THAT WOULD BE GOOD.

ENERGY

EMOTIONS

JUST BY SITTING DOWN AND
DISCUSSING THE ANSWERS
WILL BE MAJOR BREAK THROUGH
FOR MOST RELATIONSHIPS
WHATEVER THE OUTCOME

EMOTIONS

PEOPLE SKILLS

ONLY ONE KEY QUESTION.

PEOPLE SKILLS

DOES IT WORK FOR YOU?

SPECIFIC MOTIVATION

IF NOT

SPECIFIC MOTIVATION

**WE ALL HAVE TO MAKE CHOICES
THAT SHAPE OUR LIVES!**

LIFE FORCE   ?  ?   LIFE FORCE

RELATIONSHIPS

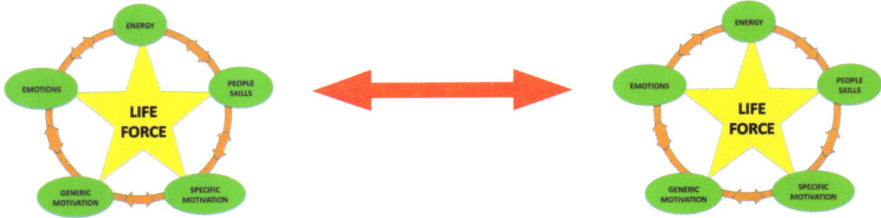

GIVE AND TAKE

In any relationship both parties are giving and taking. The question is are we HAPPY with the BALANCE BETWEEN what we have to GIVE and what we TAKE (Receive). It does not have to be equal for each individual or for that matter equal between the people in the relationship. It does have to at least be acceptable or more ideally enhance one or more of the areas in the circle and ultimately provide a deeper satisfaction and well being to our LIFE FORCE.

CHECKING THE BALANCE

Our LIFE FORCE will be constantly evaluating how all of our relationships are impacting the circle and the Life force. It will categorize the relationships with respect to importance (like maybe a Job) or how good it makes us feel (With that special person) and deciding how much we will put into the various relationships. Or indeed if the relationship is sustainable. It will make value judgments like "I will make this work" "I can put up with it" "I am out of here." This will result in actions on our SPECIFIC MOTIVATION LIST.

To check **IF** a relationship is **IN BALANCE** go through the process on the previous pages but ask slightly different questions. Only two questions for each area in the circle. What am I putting in? What am I taking out? The transaction does not have to be in the same area on the circle. For example a job will result in you providing maybe Energy and People Skills and you take in status and money which increases your wealth (Generic Motivation). This is paid employment at its simplest level. You may also take emotional strength through being employed or satisfaction from achieving specific tasks. As always everyone will be different and the LIFE FORCE will ultimately decide if the "BALANCE IS ACCEPTABLE."

"Does this work for you?"

ENJOY/GROW

TOLERATE

CHANGE

RELATIONSHIPS

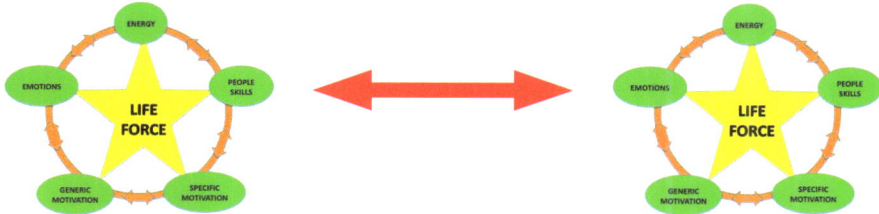

SOME REALITIES

Most of the relationships that we form are transitionary and shallow and may serve a short term purpose, then they drift away. For no other reason that other relationships move into our life. People just move on. For example, changing jobs, people we meet at events, moving house,short term membership of a club or society. This is a natural evolution in a busy world. No rights or wrongs, just the way it is. Most people know people, or situations that they were close for a time and are now in the memory bank (A nice place where no one else can go, hopefully). An occasional meeting with someone from the past maybe reminding you of the experiences.

GOOD RELATIONSHIPS

Once in a while, if we are lucky, we experience some very good relationships. Often this involves emotional Love, but could also be a particular spiritual or vocational group, or some other activity that deeply enriches our LIFE FORCE. I recently read somewhere a quote. *"Falling in Love has changed my life. It has made me realize who I am"* This has so many important features. The act of falling in love for a start (a whole separate subject) and then interestingly the love for another person that has resulted in the LIFE FORCE deeply evaluating the inner YOU. Powerful stuff. The only advice to give about these powerful, maybe life changing relationships is to enjoy them but above all WORK AT THEM. Constantly be evaluating the areas in the circle and use them to communicate and let the other person(s) realize how important this relationship is to **YOU.**

RELATIONSHIPS

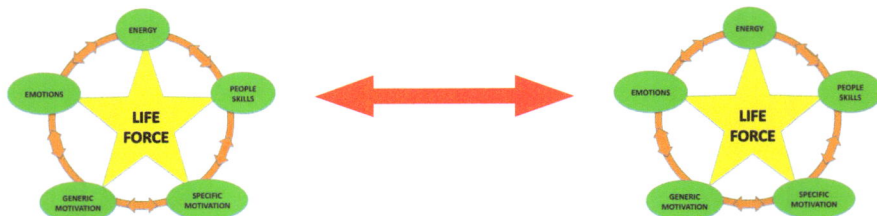

PROTECTING A RELATIONSHIP

For a relationship to survive the BALANCE between give and take has to be acceptable to all the parties. For a relationship to grow, develop and sustain a few other things may help.

Trust / Honesty / Care / Respect / Love

Awareness and empathy as to what is required.

Energy to communicate and give time, actions speak louder than words.

Compassion and support when required.

Putting the other person before you.

Avoid
INDIFFERENCE and LACK OF RESPECT.

IS THE PERSON FROM THE OTHER PLANET STILL WITH US? AND DOING THIS?

BAD RELATIONSHIPS

A bad relationship is when it makes you UNHAPPY because one or more of the areas in the circle is being depleted and your LIFE FORCE is impacted. So many people have UNHAPPY relationships. For example an abusive boss at work or an ABUSIVE or absent partner at home. So why do we put up with these relationships. Good question? Some people stay in these relationships until their LIFE FORCE is actually taken away! The main reason people stay in these relationships is because the LIFE FORCE is often making one of two judgments. There is a stronger more fulfilling relationship that depends on this bad relationship, so you accept it. For example the wife in a bad marriage but who is also a mother and she puts that maternal relationship ahead of her own happiness. The other reason is that we may believe that the alternative to this bad relationship would be a lot worse. A bad boss maybe is better than no Boss and no income. To change away from a BAD RELATIONSHIP especially one that may have evolved from an initially good relationship over a long time is very, very difficult. It takes an incredibly strong LIFE FORCE to manage that change. Many people just suffer in silence and get on with it.

RELATIONSHIPS

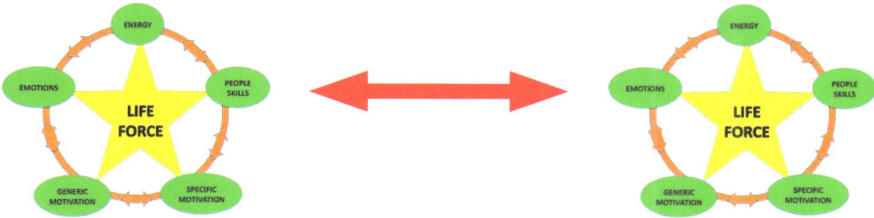

COPING WITH A BAD RELATIONSHIP

It is the same process as developing the various areas and how we react when an area is under attack. So decide which area in the CIRCLE that the relationship is damaging and use another strong area or areas in the CIRCLE to provide compensation, distraction or what ever works to cope with the situation. Some examples:

Abusive boss. You spend more time on your social life. Maybe energized to have Specific goal to find another job. Use your emotional strength and people skills to filter the bad behavior out, not let it "Get to you." Develop little amusing ways to get them, like scheduling a meeting for 6 am, reserving their seat on a plane at the back next to the toilet, it all helps pass the day! Straight faced innocence of course Ultimately change your generic motivation, move jobs if you have not managed to get the boss fired!

Abusive Partner. Throw yourself into some goal orientated tasks like work, or learning a new skill to avoid time together. Focus on the children maybe? Develop another close relationship that meets your needs. Maybe be motivated to get some professional help, counseling.

Note the term ABUSIVE is not just physical. It could be, and usually is more likely to be emotional, and verbal. This behavior usually reveals more about the inadequacies and problems of the abuser.

COMPLEXITIES OF LIFE. A SIMPLE ILLUSTRATION

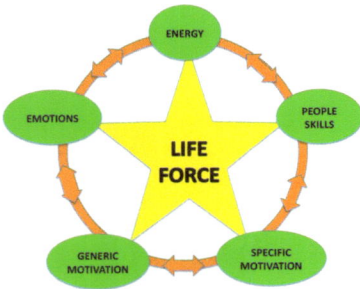

PERSON 1
MEMBER OF CLUB
DECIDES TO FIND MEMBERS
TALKS TO PERSON 2

PERSON 2
ASKED BY P1 TO JOIN THE CLUB
CONSIDERS REQUEST
AGREES TO JOIN
NOW MEMBER

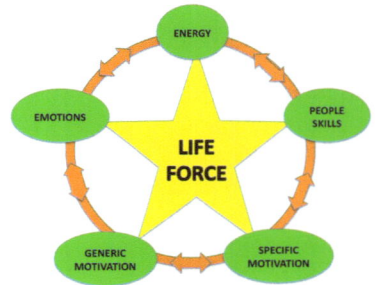

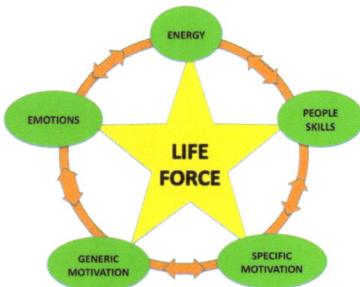

PERSON 3
SEES FLYER IN SHOP
THINKS GOOD IDEA
WANTS TO JOIN CLUB
CALLS CLUB ENROLLS
NOW MEMBER

END RESULT 3 MEMBERS IN CLUB TOGETHER.
LINKED BY GENERIC MOTIVATION

COMPLEXITIES OF LIFE

In order for this simple process to work so many things are taking place in the THREE PEOPLES LIFE FORCES.

PERSON 1

This person has to be able and willing to be in the club in the first place. (Specific and Generic Motivation). They have to think that it is a good idea to go and find other members. (Emotional desire). Then they have to have the specific motivation to do it and the Energy to make it happen. The plan to talk to person 2 involves people skills maybe a selling process. Putting a flyer in the window requires specific motivation and energy, pay for it your self. Generic Motivation.

PERSON 2

Person 2 when approached has to have a sympathetic response and the people skills to even listen in the first place. How often do we just walk past people trying to talk to us? The request has been noted and the LIFE FORCE has to evaluate it against all the 5 Areas to decide if this is a good idea. Will joining the club enhance and support any or all of my 5 areas? Will it be rewarding? Do I have the ENERGY , TIME and money (Generic Motivation) to join? If the answer to all these questions is positive then the person has to be specifically motivated to call the club and use their people skills to join. This could be an instant to say YES or maybe will take some time to consider.

PERSON 3

Person 3 has to go through a similar process to PERSON 2 but they then have to read the flyer and then they have to decide to process the same decisions as person 2.

LIFE FORCE ROLE

The LIFE FORCES of the three people are constantly reviewing this process with respect to "Is this right for me?" The LIFE FORCE controls the timing and decision process and is constantly checking if the 5 areas are going to enrich or damage me. For example the following questions may result in a negative answer. Do I have the money and time? Do I want to be a member? Do I like the people in the club? Am I fit enough to do what the club expects. Will I fit in and be liked and accepted. What's in it for me?? So many factors that could stop this process. Our LIFE FORCES could process this decision sometimes instantly or maybe think about it forever? It will depend upon where our LIFE FORCE is in managing our life. Plus what other activities are going on in our life. It is about priorities.

THIS IS ONE SMALL EXAMPLE OF THE MANY TRANSACTIONS THAT ARE BEING PROCESSED ALL THE TIME. NO WONDER DEALING WITH PEOPLE CAN BE COMPLEX?

TEAM WORK

This section uses the Circle of DEPENDENCY as an aid to TEAM BUILDING and to help understand how teams work. We are all in many teams of different types in a life time. In work groups, in social groups and as family members. Any group of people with a common purpose or goal should be considered to be a team.

TEAM DEVELOPMENT

KEY AREAS TO FOCUS

GENERIC MOTIVATION

Environment is OK? The basic facilities are fit for purpose?
Basic reward systems are sound?
Clothing or Kit provides a sense of identity?

ENERGY

Team is Fit?
Training programs meet requirements?
Preventative programs in to reduce illness?

EMOTIONS

Good attitudes?
No favorites / Jealousies / Everyone treated equally?

PEOPLE SKILLS

Team able to take, accept and interpret instruction?
Team able to communicate with each other?
Team able to communicate with anyone outside if required?

SPECIFIC MOTIVATION

Are the goals and objectives well understood and accepted?
Are there incentives in place for good performance?

LIFE FORCE

THE DEEP MOTIVATIONAL CHALLENGE.
INSTILL THE WILL TO WIN.
CREATE TEAM SPIRIT.

TEAM WORK

The purpose of TEAM is create an output that is greater than
the individual parts.

SUPER TEAMS

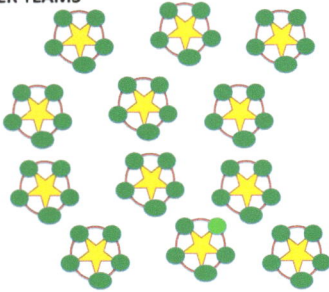

These are the teams where all the KEY AREAS
are aligned. They consequently have a strong
LIFE FORCE and the SPECIFIC MOTIVATION
is collectively focused.

WEAK TEAM MEMBER

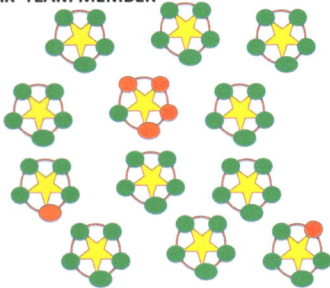

No team is perfect. The challenge for the
TEAM and its leader is to find out where the
weak links are. Then to either correct them
through training or replace them. Meanwhile
the rest of the TEAM has to develop techniques to cover this
hopefully isolated weakness.

PROBLEM TEAMS

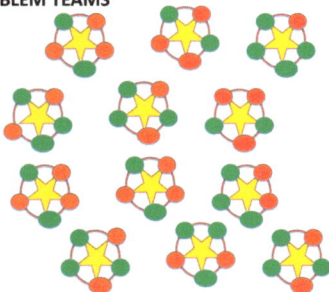

This is a major challenge that requires
STRUCTURAL ATTENTION. For this number
of team members to have this amount of KEY
AREAS going down means something is wrong
with the structure, not the individual team
members. Find out what it is and put it right.

PROBLEMS

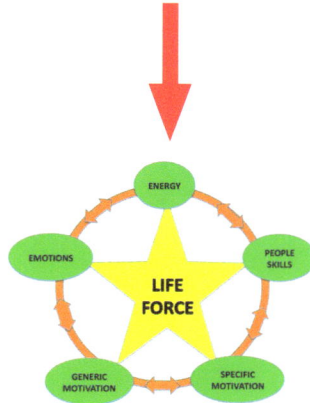

Life can deal some bad cards and problems arise. When a problem arrives it impacts the CIRCLE OF DEPENDENCY in one or more areas. When this happens it is important to take a quick review of the impact and decide a course of action. This will involve using the strength of the CIRCLE OF DEPENDENCY and also making sure that the circle is not breached to the extent that the LIFE FORCE starts to diminish. A strong LIFE FORCE will over see the defense. The LIFE FORCE mantra will kick in "I CAN DEAL WITH THIS"

VIRTUALLY ALL PROBLEMS INVOLVE THE LOSS OF SOMETHING.

FOLLOWING A LOSS WE GO THROUGH THE FOLLOWING STAGES

SHOCK . . . . .This has happened to ME!

ANGER . . . . .Why has this happened to ME?

DEPRESSION . . . . . .Poor ME?

ACCEPTANCE . . . . . .OK Better get on with it!

This process can take seconds or a life time?

THE NEXT FEW PAGES COVER THREE POTENTIALLY SERIOUS PROBLEMS

PROBLEM

END OF A CLOSE RELATIONSHIP
Make sure that it is over.
Do not do anything rash too quickly.
It may be expensive to recover.
It may also hinder /prevent any recovery
Be careful what you say and to whom.

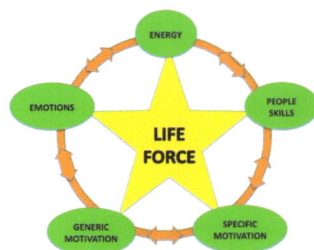

GENERIC MOTIVATION

POTENTIAL DAMAGE	POTENTIAL HELP
Difficult if in the same social group	Stay objective. Keep the high ground. Do not get into negative comments about the other person. Does not help
May involve splitting wealth.	Maybe require a third party to arbitrate. Could be a lawyer but expensive.
Re-locating change of house/ location / country.	Friends may help in the short term. But only so much. They will have their own lives to get on with. Opportunity to go somewhere you have always wanted to live.

ENERGY

POTENTIAL DAMAGE	POTENTIAL HELP
The emotional impact may cause you to be lethargic and reduce your desire to do anything energetic	Get out and do something physical. Depending upon your level of fitness of course. A long walk, intense work out. Keep focused on your body No extra eating or Drinking
Physical Harm	Hospital

EMOTIONS

POTENTIAL DAMAGE

Potentially serious damage.
Depression, anger, frustration.
A potentially serious direct hit at
your emotional "Heart Land"

POTENTIAL HELP

Time. Unfortunately is maybe the best solution. But talking to friends, focusing on developing some of the positive emotions. Try and smile, be happy. Think of things that make you happy. Do them. Life does go on for most of us. Trust your LIFE FORCE to sort it out.

PEOPLE SKILLS

POTENTIAL DAMAGE

Loss of confidence.
Loss of respect .
No skills to find another
relationship.

POTENTIAL HELP

Stay cool, take time just be you! Get out and meet people. Things happen in the most unusual ways. Be patient.

Maybe use the time to gain a skill like cooking or learn a new language. You will meet people as well.

SPECIFIC MOTIVATION

POTENTIAL DAMAGE

May have to change plans.
Common areas of interest
may not seem the same

POTENTIAL HELP

Set goals and change things
Do not rush into anything too structurally
changing. Reflect and adjust.

LIFE FORCE

**Use inner strengths
to discover YOU.
Realize that life will go on
and that other relationships
will develop.**

PROBLEM

LOSS OF A JOB
Paid employment is a an activity
It does not validate who YOU are!
Despite what you may think?

GENERIC MOTIVATION

POTENTIAL DAMAGE

Lose of income
effect life style.
Financial future
Loss of respect and esteem
Loss of friends.
No where to go and and hide
from the rest of your life?

POTENTIAL HELP

Friends and family provide support
May produce contacts for another job.
State financial support.

ENERGY

POTENTIAL DAMAGE

Feeling lethargic.
Depression.

POTENTIAL HELP

Exercise to let of steam.
Endorphin flow,
More time to get fit.
Enjoy exercise
Opportunity to travel.
Energy to apply for other jobs.

EMOTIONS

POTENTIAL DAMAGE	POTENTIAL HELP
Frozen by depression?	Seek placement help
Angry at rejection.	Talk to friends.
Grief through a loss?	Take time to reflect and renew.
Wanting to get even.	Could be a good idea.
	Wanted to leave.

PEOPLE SKILLS

POTENTIAL DAMAGE	POTENTIAL HELP
Feeling of rejection	Try to negotiate good exit package.
Reduced social interactions.	Never accept first offer. Ask for other benefits.
	Be positive and assertive.
	Interviewing skills for another job.

SPECIFIC MOTIVATION

POTENTIAL DAMAGE	POTENTIAL HELP
Loss of things to do.	Review all past goals see if any opportunities.
Action list reduced.	Redefine LIFE GOALS not just work goals.
Lose sense of purpose.	They should be different.

LIFE FORCE → **Putting "PAID EMPLOYMENT" into perspective. Plotting the way ahead. Maybe a new job or a change of life style.**

PROBLEM

SEVERE ILLNESS / INJURY
Evaluate how serious?
Evaluate how permanent?
Remain positive!

GENERIC MOTIVATION

POTENTIAL DAMAGE

Lose job.
Lose income.
Have to be relocated.
Lose friends and social life

POTENTIAL HELP

Support from friends and family.
State support financially

ENERGY

POTENTIAL DAMAGE

Lose physical fitness.
Unable to do simple tasks.
Permanent life changing damage.

POTENTIAL HELP

Create compensating work out routines
Stay disciplined on food and drink

EMOTIONS

POTENTIAL DAMAGE

Feel unloved
Brain function may be affected
Judgment may be affected.
Medications may affect
mental state.
Middle of the night is lonely
Increased insecurity.

POTENTIAL HELP

Try to put things in perspective.
Specialist professional help.
Medical?
Try and retain optimism

PEOPLE SKILLS

POTENTIAL DAMAGE

Loss of confidence.
Out of contact with friends.
They may move on and ignore you.

POTENTIAL HELP

Bond with people who may
have the same condition
Discuss emotional reaction
with friends.
Join a support group.

SPECIFIC MOTIVATION

POTENTIAL DAMAGE

A major review of plans

POTENTIAL HELP

Seek specialist help and support.
Plan for the recovery.

LIFE FORCE → **Coming to terms with the
situations and that your life
may never be the same again.
Plotting a new way ahead for you.**

THE CIRCLE OF DEPENDENCY UNDER ATTACK

We are under attack on a regular basis. Guess where most of it is coming from?
Our nearest and dearest, the people closest to us.

INCOMING ATTACKS

Criticism, made to feel of no value, ignored, not respected, not listened to, opinions ignored, opinions not asked for, shouted at, rumors spread about us, what you do is not appreciated, unreasonable demands on you, forgetting important dates, no gifts, not saying thank you,not turning up for meetings, not answering calls, not doing something they agreed to, physical violence, emotional and verbal abuse, theft or damage to property, always having to pay, someone charging stuff to you.

ON A BAD DAY YOU MAY RECEIVE SEVERAL OF THE ABOVE.

Most of these attacks are of course trivial and the stuff of life.
Just what we have to put up with in a crazy world. The KEY QUESTION.

Are these attacks IMPACTING YOUR LIFE FORCE?
Are they GETTING TO YOU?

If not just shrug your shoulders, "C'est la vie" and move on, If they are getting
to you then you should analyze these actions under one of three areas
(Thinking in threes works at so many levels.) These are detailed on
the opposite page together with some suggested counter measures.

Just before we leave this page one question.
What was your part, if any, in causing the attack?

You should also recognize that this type of behavior is often either a reaction or a way of masking a much deeper problem within the person who is attacking you. So maybe go past the symptoms and think what may have caused the attack. It may be you? Quite often this type of behavior is not just one sided. But it can be. Think about it.
If the attacks are long term and abusive. See the section on BAD RELATIONSHIPS.

DEALING WITH ATTACKS

LIFE GETTING IN THE WAY
Some people some of the time are just crazy busy or an event blows
them off course resulting in them forgetting to do something or they
have to bump you off the priority list for a short while

COUNTER MEAURE
Ask your self. Is it personal, is it a trend or a one off, has their action really caused that
much damage to me? If the answers are favorable just move on. Get over it.

IT IS THE WAY THEY ARE?
This is where the person attacking is made that way. Short temper, aggressive,
low tolerance. What ever. They maybe do not mean it and it is not personal.

COUNTER MEAURE
Again the key question. Does this work for you and are you prepared to put up with this
behavior? Analyze what is causing the behavior because it is often one of their problems
being taken out on you. Insecure people often attack and criticize others. Frustrated
people often use aggression to relieve their frustrations. Also is this a short term issue or
endemic behavior. Choices may have to be made. Up to you. As always.

DELIBERATE CRUEL BEHAVIOR
Sad fact of life is that there are some people who just like attacking other people. They
enjoy it and you may just be a victim. You may even be in a relationship that is slowly un-
folding to reveal the true nature of the other person. This is true in both personal life and
the work place. It is not that unusual to come across managers with serious problems
and where their actions damage people on a regular and systematic basis.

COUNTER MEAURE
The quick answer is get out and leave them to it.
This is not always possible of course. The relationship section has some ideas on how to
handle an abusive relationship. These people need help so try and find a way of getting
it to them.Ultimately the best solution is go and find a better situation. Retaliation normally
just feeds the bad behavior unless totally preemptive. For example getting the boss fired.
It can be done.

DEFENDING ATTACKS FROM 5 AREAS

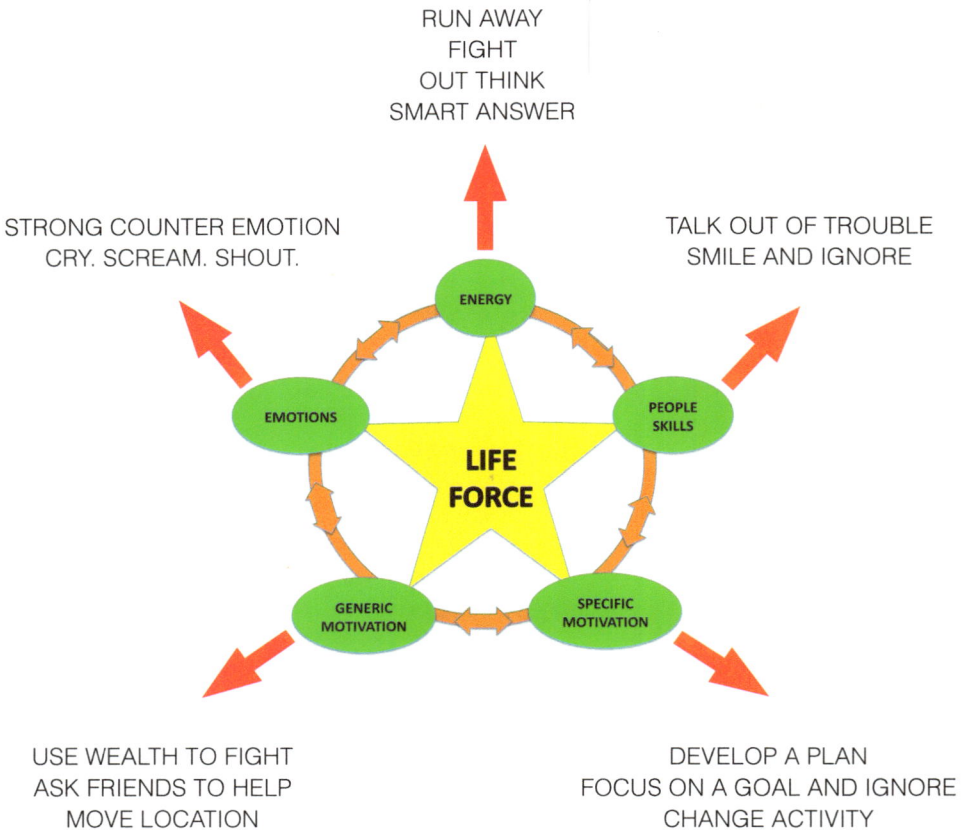

RUN AWAY
FIGHT
OUT THINK
SMART ANSWER

STRONG COUNTER EMOTION
CRY. SCREAM. SHOUT.

TALK OUT OF TROUBLE
SMILE AND IGNORE

ENERGY

EMOTIONS

PEOPLE SKILLS

LIFE FORCE

GENERIC MOTIVATION

SPECIFIC MOTIVATION

USE WEALTH TO FIGHT
ASK FRIENDS TO HELP
MOVE LOCATION

DEVELOP A PLAN
FOCUS ON A GOAL AND IGNORE
CHANGE ACTIVITY

Some of the defenses may involve more than one area and could be complex. A simple example would be crying that could involve, EMOTIONS, ENERGY, and PEOPLE SKILLS. Or we may use our ENERGY to stop crying, or not cry because we do not want anyone to see that they have got to us. Or we may reverse that to let them know that they may have gone too far. Plus are we crying for pleasure or pain?

IN SOME ATTACKS DEPLOY THE MOST POWERFUL SENTENCE.

NO.

SERIOUS ATTACK THE CIRLE IS BREACHED AND THE AREAS OVER RUN

LIFE FORCE

AREAS OVER RUN LIFE FORCE TAKES OVER

REVIEWS ALL AREAS AND ESTABLISHES DAMAGE.

SEEKS ANOTHER PERSON TO PROVIDE BACK UP.

CHECKS INTO RECOVERY PROGRAM / MEDICAL HELP.

SEEKS DEEP SPIRITUAL GUIDANCE .

RELEASE ADRENALIN TO RECHARGE THE AREAS.

WITHDRAWS TO REFLECT AND RECOVER

REVIEWS MEMORY BANK SEE IF ANY IDEAS TO HELP

CHECKS IF ANY AREAS CAN BE STARTED UP AGAIN.

DEVELOPS A RECOVERY PLAN

EXTREME CASES.
NOT ABLE TO RECOVER.
JUST GIVES UP AND WAITS / HOPES FOR RESCUE?

DIFFICULT AREAS

These two pages deal with some difficult areas. People whose life Force is so low that they are in a state of total despair and maybe they are considering ending it. Some years back I worked for an organization that provided voluntary help for people in despair and who were contemplating suicide. I have sat with people at the worst moments of their life and have talked to people a few hours before they have actually ended their LIFE. I thought long and hard about putting this section in but I thought maybe someone may take some points from this and it could help another person. You never know.

PEOPLE IN TOTAL DESPAIR. SOME OBSERVATIONS

People at the lowest level often have a total lack of interest in anything. They are not aware of the world around them. It is as though their LIFE FORCE has just gone out. I have sat with someone for a couple of hours and they were staring ahead and kept repeating "Why me" I was not in the room as far as that person was concerned.

Some important points from this situation.

Be very concerned if some one has absolutely no interest in anything especially you.

Sometimes people are so low that they do not even have the ENERGY to kill themselves. One of the danger times to watch for with people in this condition is when they are starting to recover and get some energy back. Hopefully it is the start of the recovery. But it could also create enough energy to end their life.

Listen, Listen, Listen. Ask open questions to encourage them to tell you how they feel.

Do not give them any advice. Unless it is specific and factual.

Do not say, anything like "Pull yourself together" this will only increase their sense of inadequacy as they will not be able to do it. This is for seriously depressed people not someone just having a bad day when this may work.

Encourage them to find some professional help.

Recognize that you usually cannot fix the problem. Just be there for them.

Recognize that for some people this is an illness that requires to be treated. It is not just life getting them down.

DIFFICULT AREAS

Do not react to anything they may say, especially about you.
They probably do not mean it.

Be empathetic but keep your energy up. Do not go in there with them. It will
deplete you and they are depending upon your energy to give them some strength.
Keep your areas high they will be taking.

Do not say anything that in better times you may regret. For example if the situation is as a
result of a break up with a partner. Do not say I never liked that person anyway. They were
no good for you. Guess where that puts you when they are all back together and happy
again. Maybe lost a friend. You never really know what is going on in a relationship.

Try not to avoid the person because it depresses YOU. Hopefully this is a temporary
period in their life and you may be able to help them to get through it.
You are not expected to have a magic solution.

Try and encourage them to talk to an independent person, maybe a councilor or therapist. People at times of despair often tell a close friend deep feelings and secrets about
themselves that when they are better regret having said. Friends can be lost like this. If the
person does not want to go deep, do not interrogate to get to the bottom of what's wrong!

DEALING WITH GRIEF
For many people who get to this low point it is as a result of the loss of a loved partner,
a close friend or family member. Losing a child can be the most devastating
situation that a person may have to face up to. If a loss is the cause of the
persons' condition then all of the general points above still apply but a
couple of special ones for dealing with this loss and grief.

If the person wants to talk about the person they have lost, let them.
They usually do but so many people have difficulty dealing with this as
they are often dealing with their own grief. Do not change the subject.

Understand the process that they are going through. Shock, Anger, Depression,
Acceptance, Recovery. Do not try and get them through this quickly. They have to take
their own time. Some people may stay at the depressed stage for a long time.

No one usually ever "Gets over" the serious loss of a very close person.
They just earn to live the loss.

THIS IS A VERY SERIOUS AREA. BE A FRIEND.
BUT MAYBE? SEEK PROFESSIONAL HELP.

FEAR

WORRY

Fear usually leads to worry and that in turn may lead to anxiety and that in turn may lead to depression. So many people are impacted by depression that originates in a basic FEAR of something that **"may happen"**. We all worry about something at some time, it is a matter of degree. Some people are just natural worriers. They are made that way. Deep in their LIFE FORCE is an emotional component that causes them to worry. Worry is basically how they will react to or be affected by the FEAR of something that may happen. We have to help the LIFE FORCE overcome this emotional reaction by applying some logic and reasoning. Studies have shown that of the various things that we worry about over 90% never happen. Of the 10% or less of things that do happen most of them are no where near as bad as we expected, of the few things that we worry about that do happen and become catastrophic events in our life there was usually not a lot we could have done to prevent them happening. They were going to happen anyway. An overwhelmingly conclusive logical case to never worry about anything ever again. So stop worrying. Of course this will not work. Since when has logic and reasoning ever defeated emotions and feelings? So a couple of tips to help.

NEVER GIVE BIRTH TO WORRY

When ever a FEAR about something that COULD happen starts to develop in your head. Stop it. Do not tell anyone else as this will give the thought a life. Maybe some one else is now worrying, not only about the subject, but also about you being worried. If you do say it out loud then it is out there and has to be dealt with. People may ask you about it and it gains life. Potentially a very debilitating life that will attack your LIFE FORCE.

REPLACE A WORRY

One of the ways to stop the worry at birth in your head is to replace it with another more positive thought. Keep in your head a library of nice thoughts. A good experience or maybe a beautiful object like an image of a sunflower?

THESE IDEAS ARE VERY DIFFICULT TO DO.
THEY WORK MOST OF THE TIME FOR ME.

PROCEED AND EMBRACE LIFE. DO NOT WORRY.

BE FEARLESS.

JEALOUSY / ENVY.

Though shall not covet they neighbors goods. — Why Not?

After all is this not what makes the world go round us aspiring to own goods that we see some one else with. One of the central themes of a capitalist society is that we are defined by our ownership of goods. It is a statement about who we are and maybe how successful we are. No one buys a Rolex watch because they need to know the time.

It is a fine line between admiring and wanting as a motivation to achieve something as against being resentful and jealous that someone has something that you do not have.

Jealousy possibly one of the most destructive emotions. Quote "jealousy is the root of all evil. It normally replies to relationships and can occur in family groups, in the work place, in romantic relationships and even between friendly platonic relationships. Our emotions are typically driven by a fear of loss of what we have to someone else and it is a most common human condition and can lead to anger, resentment, depression, Fear, and possibly violence.

Envy is a similar emotion to Jealousy and is often used in the same context. It does however have some subtle differences. Envy can in some ways be positive as admiration that motivates you to become like the person who you admire. More typically envy leads to more negative thoughts as it could be contrasted to Jealousy where as Envy is desiring something we do not have. As against being jealous of losing something we already may have, like the loss of a friend to someone else.

UNDERSTAND AND ACCEPT
Life is not fair.
Most of the negative thoughts are generated from within you.
The emotions that you feel are causing you more damage than the other person.

DEALING WITH JEALOUSY & ENVY
Build and develop your own self confidence.
Accept that you are what you are.
Do not get hung up on materialism.
Love and forgive those that wish you harm.
Accept that life will be what it will be for the most part.

GIVING ADVICE
First a bit of general advice....Don't.

LET ME EXPLAIN

I think that giving advice is tempting and could be requested in three areas. A subject or hobby of mutual interest, About another person, About another person's partner of friends. Let us explore each one.

SPECIALIST SUBJECT

If you happen to be a photographer and meet another photographer and they ask how to do something and really want to know? Go for it, bond and share knowledge. If you're sitting next to a person who casually asks about photography because you have a camera (always a clue) then decide if it is just polite conversation or do they really want to know. Interest can move quickly to losing the will to live.

ABOUT THE OTHER PERSON.
Que. Does this outfit suit me?
Thinks. Absolutely not. It's hideous and makes you look fat.
Ans. Great but I prefer.....(almost anything!)
Point: The "Truth does not always set you free."
It can actually get you into some trouble!

ABOUT ANOTHER PERSON'S PARTNER? FRIEND

Never give an opinion especially if asked? Especially if they say "I would like you to be honest with me, I really would like to know." Relationships are complex and you never know what is going on, so keep out. However If the visitor from the other planet has now left and you feel the need to let a friend know what you think then some ways of doing it maybe? Ask some open questions to make them think about their actions. Maybe using another person as an example, maybe your self. Your friend will have to work out what works for them by themselves. With or without your advice. Example questions:

How do you feel about that person? Do they make you really happy?

I heard about a friend the other day who was going round with this great person, guess what they turned out to be???

I had a great weekend ?? Really good having a partner that respects my freedom and lets me do my own thing, I am so lucky. Maybe?

Where ever you can ask open questions that make some one think. We all have to get there in our own way and learn through personal experience, not being told what to do. However if some one asks you for a specific piece of information and you know the answer, tell them. For example Que What time is the next train. Ans 10.45. Not "What time do you think it is?"

A PERSPECTIVE

I was in a restaurant discussing this book with a friend and
the server came up and we were engrossed in conversation and
in our own little world. He tried to get our attention and
we said something, not sure what. He replied.

I do not look, I do not judge I just serve!

I said brilliant, what a great life skill!.
That's is going in my book. Of course he did not believe me.

Thank you Adam. That says it all!

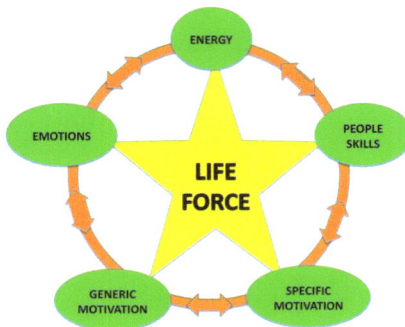

CONCLUDING THOUGHTS

I sincerely hope that you enjoyed the book. If in the unlikely event that you are going down the road of thinking that this may be an academic or intellectual analysis at any level, please stop. This is just a collection of my thoughts and experiences gained through meeting many people in all walks of life and in several countries. No more or no less.

I have found that if you go out and embrace life and meet people, things happen. Usually good things but not always. There are some nasty folks out there. If you are constantly striving to find the **"Meaning of Life"** maybe you should not waste all that time and energy because great brains for centuries have all tried and failed.

We may never find out what it is all about but one thing is absolutely certain that regardless of what the answer may be "We are all in this world together."I believe the challenge for all of us is to create a **"Meaningful Life"** and to help our fellow travellers to do the same along the way.

If you take just a few ideas a way from this book that help you to become more of what you want to be and develop some skills to help other people become more of what they want to be, that's great. Job done.

A TRUE STORY!

CHARMAINE

When I was writing this book I went to stay in a hotel for a few days, and visited the lounge where the hostess was a young lady called Charmaine. As usual, I asked how are you and where did you get that name from as it was not a local one. She said that her parents had named her after a song and that one day she would find out all about it. So I just popped over to the computer, hit the internet, and printed a one page history of the song and gave it to her. Her face really lit up, I mean really lit up, and I just said "Great, enjoy!" and left. Guess what sort of service I had for the next few days. A few free drinks genuinely treated really well like a long lost friend. What a great investment for about 5 minutes of consideration. As I was writing this book I came back on the second day and watched how the various people treated Charmaine when they entered the lounge. Everyone had to make contact and sign in. The results really surprised me. I observed 40 people, all ages, sexes and probably 5 or so different countries. Most people were polite, respectful and said please and thank you in the right place. Two I defined as just rude. This is the real surprising fact, not one person mentioned her name despite, it being on a badge. Five people did make some nice pleasant conversation and showed an interest in her which she appreciated. For the other 35 people she was just someone sitting behind a desk. I have absolutely no idea on the statistical relevance of this sample if you include me? Only 1 person in 41 mentioned her name. Depressing at so many levels.

THE POINT

For an investment of a few minutes of my time my experience in that hotel was better and cost me less money. This is the real good one. Every time I went in the lounge she would beam and smile and say how are you today Mr. Moore, most people in there would look up and maybe think "Who is that guy, he must be important." So payback in kind. How come 40 people did not make any effort to do the same. How come 40 people did not know that ONE WORD was the key to free drinks, superior service and being made to feel special. I was tempted not to put this little secret in the book so I sneaked it in at the back. Would not like too much competition. I know you will not believe this! Just as I was finishing that sentence Charmaine came across the lounge beaming and said "How are you tonight Mr. Moore?" I said great I am just writing about you in my book. She smiled and walked away not believing it for one minute. But that is a whole other point about why she did not believe me. It is in the way you tell it.

THREE PIECES OF ADVICE

MY BARBER

Not the usual type of barber as he had spent over 40 years reading every book that he could find on religion, philosophy, ethics and related subjects. So I asked him one day "Why all the books." He explained that he had set out when he was 20 to find out what it was all about. "So?" I asked. "Two conclusions" he said.

He still did not know what it was all about?
BUT
No one else did either!

HOLLYWOOD

Watching a movie the leading lady was thinking of going to see a therapist. She hesitated, in, then out, then in, then finally out. Just before she left she asked the Therapist, "Is there any general advice that you would give that deals with most situations?" Yes he replied.

Decide what you want in this life. Then find a way of asking for it.

THE PSYCHIATRISTS

I was recently having dinner with a group of psychiatrists, socially he quickly added, and we were just chatting about the meaning of life as they have experience of so many mental conditions. So I asked if they had reached any conclusions? Yes they replied.

You enter this world alone and you leave it alone. You have to
decide who you want to spend the time with when you are here?

VOLTAIRE (1694 -1778)
Doubt is not a pleasant condition, but certainty is absurd!

THE VIOLINIST

Two people were sitting in the front row of a concert being given by a world class violinist. The music was superb and very emotional. One person turned to the other person and said "have you seen the hole in the violinists sock" Of course this said more about the person than the violinist.

When ever you are in contact with anyone on this planet let your LIFE FORCE do the communicating.

LISTEN TO THE MUSIC

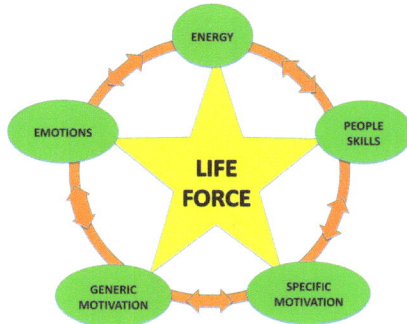

DIFFERENT PEOPLE. HOW THEY MAY LOOK. MAYBE?

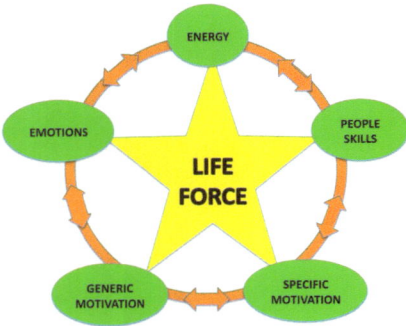

HAPPY WELL BALANCED
EVERYTHING GOING WELL

**THE VISITOR FROM
ANOTHER PLANET.**

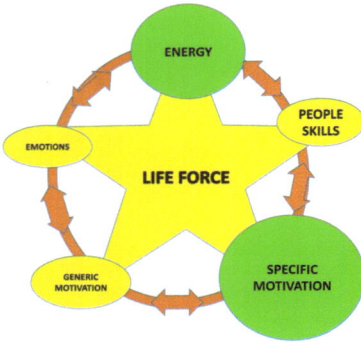

HIGH ACHIEVER.
BIG ENERGY.
NO INTEREST IN PEOPLE.
LOW EMOTIONAL PROFILE.

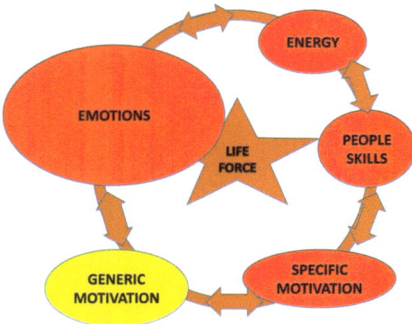

OH DEAR !
EVERYTHING GOING WRONG.
SERIOUSLY DEPRESSED.

HOW ABOUT YOU

NOW

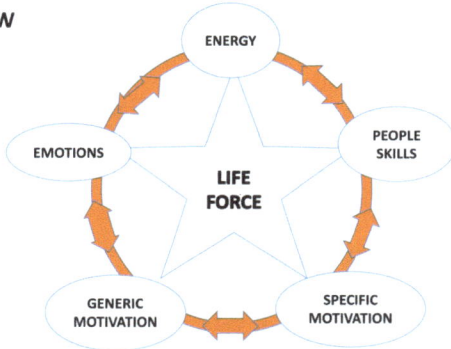

THREE ACTIONS TO GET THERE

_____

_____

_____

HOW I WOULD LIKE TO BE

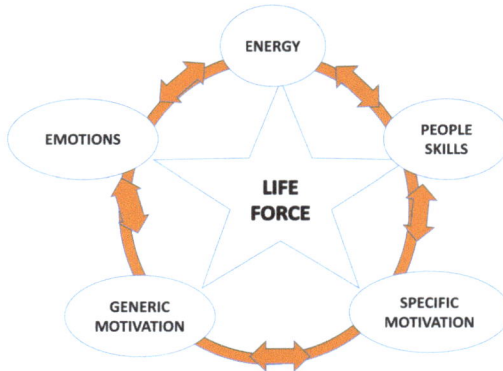

OTHER BOOKS BY BRIAN MOORE

A DAY WITH A CEO HANDBOOK

A Day With a CEO is a handbook for General Managers outlining the key requirements for the job of GM. It covers the things you need to know to effectively provide leadership and vision and oversee all functional areas of a business. Inside the book you will find several checklists and over 100 ideas on how to increase profit. Although targeted at General Managers, A Day With a CEO is a valuable resource for anyone interested in how a business should be managed, especially early career managers with aspirations to become a GM.

CreateSpace eStore: https://www.createspace.com/3864845

FINANCE FOR THE GENERAL MANAGER

Authored by Brian Moore, Authored by Michelle Jeffrey

Finance for the General Manager is the second book in the A Day With a CEO series. It focuses on FINANCE, which is the most important area that any GM requires to understand because a BUSINESS HAS THE MAIN OBJECTIVE OF MAKING MONEY. How that money is created and recorded in a set of accounts is fundamentally important. The book includes detailed exercises that have been simplified to ease the understanding of financial concepts and exercises and schematics to help understand business finance. Although targeted at GMs, the content will be useful to anyone interested in how a business should be managed.

CreateSpace eStore: https://www.createspace.com/3924915

PEOPLE

This third book in the A Day With a CEO series focuses on PEOPLE as the successful inspiring, leading and motivating of people is absolutely fundamental to the success of any organization. Many of the subjects covered in this book are often described as the soft skills of management, as anyone who deals with people on a regular basis will tell you that this is one of the hardest aspects of the job. Although targeted at General Managers, the content will be useful to anyone interested in how a business should be managed, especially early career managers with aspirations to become a GM.

CreateSpace eStore: https://www.createspace.com/3925276